PRAISE FOR
THE CHRISTIAN MAN

A lot of people talk about how hard it is to be a man today. But Patrick Morley took things a step farther and actually asked men about the pain points in their lives. The result is a powerful guide for guys who want to become godly men—but aren't quite sure where to start.

Dave Ramsey, bestselling author and nationally syndicated radio show host

No one knows more about Christian manhood than Pat Morley. In this one-of-a-kind book, he's passing on to you the very best of what he has learned during several decades of working with men. Read this watershed book, and you will have everything you need to passionately love God, protect and provide for your family, and courageously stay the course while experiencing contentment, peace, and joy.

Dr. Tony Evans, president of The Urban Alternative and senior pastor of Oak Cliff Bible Fellowship

Very few people speak to the soul of men like Patrick Morley. His words are real and raw and redemptive. You will be challenged and encouraged as you read.

Mark Batterson, *New York Times* bestselling author of *The Circle Maker* and lead pastor of National Community Church

Open the table of contents and look at the topics—this speaks straight to the core issues men are wrestling with, in that straightforward, honest, biblical style Patrick is so well-known for. I think you'll find this book to be very encouraging.

John Eldredge, author of *Wild at Heart*

THE
CHRISTIAN MAN

THE CHRISTIAN MAN

A CONVERSATION ABOUT THE
10 ISSUES MEN SAY MATTER MOST

PATRICK MORLEY

ZONDERVAN

The Christian Man
Copyright © 2019 by Patrick Morley

Requests for information should be addressed to:
Zondervan, *3900 Sparks Dr. SE, Grand Rapids, Michigan 49546*

ISBN 978-0-310-35606-6 (international trade paper)

ISBN 978-0-310-35610-3 (audio)

Library of Congress Cataloging-in-Publication Data

Names: Morley, Patrick M., author.
Title: The Christian man : a conversation about the 10 issues men say matter
   most / Patrick Morley.
Description: Grand Rapids, Michigan : Zondervan, [2019] | Includes
   bibliographical references.
Identifiers: LCCN 2019003597 | ISBN 9780310356004 (hardcover) | ISBN
   9780310356097 (ebook)
Subjects: LCSH: Christian men--Religious life. | Men--Religious life. | Christian
   men--Conduct of life. | Men--Conduct of life.
Classification: LCC BV4528.2 .M6638 2019 | DDC 248.8/42--dc23
LC record available at https://lccn.loc.gov/2019003597

Published in association with the literary agency of Wolgemuth & Associates, Inc.

Cover design: Studio Gearbox
Cover concept: Brian Russell
Cover illustration: Spencer Creative Co. / Lightstock
Interior design: Kait Lamphere

Printed in the United States of America

20 21 22 23 24 25 26 /LSC/ 15 14 13 12 11 10 9 8 7 6 5 4 3 2

To Robert Wolgemuth—
literary agent, bestselling author,
husband, father, and my friend—

*Robert launched my writing career
and has continued to guide and manage me from day one.*

And

to Chuck Mitchell—
business owner, real estate professional,
husband, father, and my friend—

*Chuck has managed my business interests
with such skill that I've been free to
pursue ministry to men full-time.*

*   *   *

To work with a colleague whose skill, integrity, humility, perseverance, and wisdom are the first qualities that come to mind is silver. To work with such a man for your entire career is gold. But to be able to work with two such men and also to call them friends—that's platinum. That privilege has been mine. You both are phenomenal examples of *the Christian man.*

Thanks, guys.

A SPECIAL ACKNOWLEDGMENT

I want to especially thank and honor the twenty-four men who met with me as a group to decide which issues they thought had enough gravitas to be in this book.

Danny Alvarez	Steve Jones
Nicholas Angelakos	Daniel Kinney
Nick Augello	Jesse Lugo
Joshua Brockman	Marcos Peres
Nathan Burns	Matt Rearden
Fred Burt	Steve Rice
Lonzo Caves	Bryan Richardson
Andy Corley	Brian Russell
Brendon Dedekind	Chris Thurman
Kevan Enger	Nick Turco
Ron Gruninger	Reggie White
Steve Hall	Cedrick Williams

CONTENTS

Prologue: A Parable about Two Lions 13

A Few Things to Cover as You Begin This Book 15

1. Identity: Settling Who I Am and What My
   Life Is About 21
2. Life Balance: How to Be Faithful with Everything
   Entrusted to Me 39
3. Growth: Becoming a More Kingdom-Minded Man 63
4. Marriage: Finding a New Best Friend in My Wife 91
5. Children: A Dad Who Really Makes a Difference 111
6. Friendships: Finding and Keeping Godly Friends 131
7. Work: How Should I Think about My Work? 151
8. Lust: The Right Way to Deal with This
   Powerful Drive 171
9. Culture: The Role of a Christian Man in Our Culture . . 195
10. Sharing My Faith: Having Authentic Spiritual
    Conversations with My Friends 215

Afterword 239

Acknowledgments 243
*Appendix: Patrick Morley Books for Individual or
   Group Study* 245
Notes 249

A PARABLE ABOUT TWO LIONS

Once upon a time, a lion lived contently in a zoo. Born there, he had never known any other way of life. And it was a good life—all the red meat he could eat, regular physical exams, and fresh straw every day.

One day, another lion—one captured in the wild—was brought into the habitat. Every day, the jungle lion paced back and forth looking for a way to escape, growing more restless each passing day.

The zoo lion, unable to understand why the wild lion was so upset, asked, "Why so blue? Everything we need for a happy life we have right here. What else could you possibly want? Why do you want to escape from paradise?"

The wild lion couldn't believe his ears. How could he possibly explain freedom to a zoo lion who had never seen a jungle—a lion living in exile who thought he already had everything he could want? How could he convey that there's more to life than living like a caged animal?

In the months that followed, the jungle lion opened the zoo

lion's eyes with stories about life in the wild. The more the zoo lion heard about the jungle, the more he wanted to know. He peppered the jungle lion with questions like, "How big is it? What's it like? How do you get there from here?" and a hundred more just like those.

The jungle lion was sometimes eager, and always patient, to explain the glories of the jungle to the zoo lion who had only known captivity. Under such intentional mentoring, the zoo lion soon came to see that something about his world just wasn't right. He too became restless and longed to be free.

A FEW THINGS TO COVER AS YOU BEGIN THIS BOOK

See to it that no one takes you captive through hollow and deceptive philosophy, which depends on human tradition and the elemental spiritual forces of this world rather than on Christ.

COLOSSIANS 2:8

No man fails on purpose. Quite the opposite. When our feet hit the floor every morning, we're looking for a win.

But these are turbulent times to be a man. Most of the Christian men I talk to find it increasingly difficult to juggle all their responsibilities as men, husbands, fathers, friends, workers, churchmen, and citizens. As my friend Nick put it, "It feels almost impossible to live out a biblical model of manhood."

We all feel it, don't we? Like the zoo lion, we know that something about this world just isn't right. There are so many "hollow and deceptive" voices phishing to get inside our heads. It feels like we're being "hacked." Spiritually hacked.

Will those voices keep you from getting that win we all want? Have the "spiritual forces of this world" become so strong that you're not sure if biblical manhood is even possible?

Or is it still possible for you to passionately love God, protect and provide for your family, find satisfying work, and courageously lead a balanced life with the help of a few brothers, while experiencing meaning, contentment, peace, and joy?

The answer is a resounding yes. I want to give you a hopeful vision that you can get that win we're all looking for. God has a game plan for you to achieve biblical manhood. It's the time-tested, proven process that the Bible calls simply "making disciples."

However, just as no man fails on purpose, as my colleague Jamie says, "No man succeeds by accident." So in addition to a hopeful vision, you're also going to need the resources to make it happen. Which is why I've written this book. My goal is to pass on to you the best of what I've learned about biblical manhood during several decades of working with men as my vocation.

People urgently need—even ache—to see the radical impact that an authentic Christian man can have on everyone and everything around him. God's desire is for you to become that man.

If you are growing, want to grow, or *want* to want to grow—my prayer is that *The Christian Man* will prove to be exactly what you've been looking for.

SOMETHING UNIQUE ABOUT THIS BOOK

To make sure this book scratches where you itch, I gathered twenty-four Christian men from twenty-four to forty-seven years of age (mostly mid-thirties) on a Saturday morning to storyboard the question, "What are the issues and topics that would make you feel *compelled* to pick up and read a book for men?" These men come from all walks of life and represent the racial and ethnic diversity of America.

When the dust settled, we had a list of ten issues that mattered most. That list formed the table of contents for this book. Then I asked them, "What are the questions you would most like to have answered or addressed about each of those topics?"

Storyboarding is a democratic process of brainstorming that makes sure each participant has an equal voice to all the others. The book you are holding in your hands is what emerged from this process.

WHAT WE WON'T BE DOING

If this world is all you've ever known, you may think you have it good, but only because, like the zoo lion, you don't know what you're missing.

But then, as happened to me, one day you discover that a larger world exists beyond what you know. And you realize you will never be happy again until you fill the spiritual ache in your soul for God.

Like every other man, I started my spiritual journey unsure of myself. I was unsure of my identity in Christ. I didn't understand the religious lingo. I didn't have enough experience to know which teachings were biblical or which were just "man's best thinking" or "human tradition" on the subject. I lacked confidence.

Often, I was afraid not to believe what seemed like some crazy things. For example, a preacher on TV said that if I pledged to give God a 10 percent tithe of $10,000 next year, then I could "expect" God to give me $100,000 of income. That idea looks kooky to me now as I write it, but it really mixed me up at the time.

As a result, I was vulnerable to and taken captive by a lot of unorthodox, misleading, and destructive ideas from which I hope to spare you. That's why *The Christian Man* will not

- point out all the ways you are failing as a man
- get you amped up, jacked up, and fired up to live for Jesus in your own strength
- present Christianity as a "set of behaviors" to which you must adhere
- present you with a list of rules that, if kept, promise heaven on earth
- offer a performance-based approach to Christianity
- provide "sin management" systems to keep you from stumbling
- urge you to be the perfect Christian
- wallow in self-pity (sometimes you need a hug, sometimes a kick in the pants)
- challenge you to "man up" and self-will yourself to a standard that can't be sustained

Here's my promise. You can live a heroic life right now for the glory of Christ. In each chapter, I'll provide you with a "call to action" to help you think through how you want to respond. By the end of this book, you will know how to release the power of God on the issues that matter most to you. You'll be able to walk with confidence in the one identity that matters most: *the Christian man.*

PS: Download a complimentary digital copy of *The Christian Man Coaching Guide* at TheChristianManBook.com.

ONE

IDENTITY

Settling Who I Am and
What My Life Is About

Therefore, if anyone is in Christ, the new creation
has come: The old has gone, the new is here!

2 CORINTHIANS 5:17

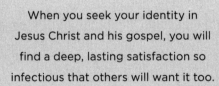

When you seek your identity in
Jesus Christ and his gospel, you will
find a deep, lasting satisfaction so
infectious that others will want it too.

THE MAN IN ROOM 3330

Word had spread throughout the hospital about Ken, the upbeat eighty-year-old man in room 3330. His buoyant, cheerful attitude was infectious among the hospital staff.

One morning, a doctor appeared at the door of his hospital room and read his chart. After looking it over, he said to Ken, "I wonder if I could talk to you for a minute." He was not one of Ken's doctors.

"Sure. What's on your mind," Ken replied.

He said, "Well, I've heard about you around the hospital, and I'd like to know how it is that you, at your age and with the difficulties you're having, can be so upbeat and cheerful?"

Ken answered, "I would be happy to tell you, but first you tell me, how do you find your enjoyment?"

"To tell you the truth," the doctor said, "I really don't have much enjoyment. I had a plane, and I thought that would do it. But that didn't work. Now we have a boat, but that doesn't seem to work either. I've got a big income. That's really brought me no lasting satisfaction. To be completely honest with you, nothing I have ever done has brought me much satisfaction."

Ken said, "I know what you're going through. In my lifetime, the only thing that I've ever found that has provided me any lasting peace and satisfaction is a relationship with Jesus Christ."

About that time, Maria, a Hispanic housekeeper about fifty years old, entered the room. Ken had spoken with her on several previous occasions. She wrung out her mop and started working on the other side of the bed from where the doctor stood.

Maria was the lowest-paid person in the hospital. She would have to work for the next twenty years to earn as much as this doctor would make in the current year.

Ken said, "Maria, can you come here, please?" She looked up, and her peaceful countenance radiated sunshine throughout the room. Then Ken said to the doctor, "I want you to look into Maria's face. She has what I'm talking about. Do you see it?"

The three of them fell quiet. The doctor looked into Maria's face. Ken and Maria alternated glances between each other and the doctor. Ken could peer into the doctor's heart. Yes, this doctor saw what Maria had. It was transparent that she had the missing thing for which he had been searching. It was clear that he wanted what Maria and Ken had found. It was a poignant spiritual moment.

"Maria," Ken finally said, "are you a follower of Christ?"

It seemed impossible, but Maria beamed even more broadly and said, "Oh yes, I love my Jesus Christ." Ken thanked her, and she continued with her chores.

The Day That Changed Ken's Life

Over the next fifteen minutes, Ken told this restless doctor that many years before, he had felt exactly the same way—no lasting peace, only short bursts of satisfaction, and no real sense of who he was or what his life was about.

"One Monday morning," he said, "I cried out to God to come into my life, forgive my sins, and give my life peace and meaning. Blinded by tears, I had to pull over to the side of the road. That morning, I put my future in the hands of Jesus Christ and asked him to show me how to live.

"All I ever asked him to give me was peace and joy. He answered my prayer, and that's why you're in here right now trying to find out what's going on. But it's not my peace and joy. It's the peace and joy of the Holy Spirit because of Jesus Christ.

"In five more minutes you'll be gone. Tomorrow I'll go home, and we'll probably never see each other again. But before you go, let me tell you the one thing that can help you. If you want what I have, what Maria has, then sometime today I want to encourage you to go find a quiet place and cry out to Jesus Christ. Tell him what's in your heart. Ask him to forgive your sins and surrender your life to him in faith. Settle it. Then you will have what Maria and I both have."

Ken's Secret

I am an eyewitness to Ken's life. We had lunch together every week for thirty-two years, and though he was thirty years my senior, we were best friends. Ken was not a "big man" in the way the world defines it. He was an ordinary, everyday kind of guy—a paint salesman—who found his greatest joy in giving his time to God and helping people.

Ken's secret was that he had settled it—who he was "in Christ" was who he really was. He was a disciple of Jesus disguised as a paint salesman. As a result, he was able to live a passionate life for the glory of God until he took his last heroic breath.

What could be more desirable? No doubt that's why the men who helped storyboard this book picked *identity* as one of their ten issues that matter most.

Let's begin by asking what motivated that doctor to seek out Ken. What did he want? He wanted what we all want!

WHAT MEN WANT

We're all wired to want three things:

A cause—something we can give our lives to that will make a difference. This is our need to be significant, to find a purpose and a mission. I have a statement written at the top of my to-do list: "I would rather die for a worthy cause than live for no reason."

A companion—someone to share life with. This is the sphere of relationships, love, family, friends, or a wife. A man goes off to hunt his bear (his cause) and then returns home to be congratulated or consoled by his wife and the community that loves and supports him.

A conviction—a belief system that explains why the first two are so difficult. *Conviction* is another word for belief system or worldview. We all want a belief system or worldview that is true and coherent and makes sense of God and life. Of the four worldviews—secular, moral, religious, and Christian—all eventually fail except Christianity, and usually at the worst possible moment. The Christian worldview is the only conviction that makes more sense as time passes. All other worldviews make less sense over time because of the unexplainable anomalies that keep piling up.

Of course, we could make a much longer list of wants—I used to keep a much longer list myself. However, by working with men as a vocation, I've discovered that once you satisfy these three wants, everything else you want (and need) generally falls into line.

The difference between Ken and the doctor was their conviction. Second Corinthians 5:17 reads, "Therefore, if anyone is in Christ, the new creation has come: The old has gone, the new is here!"

Ken embraced Christ and his gospel. His "old" conviction— the "hollow and deceptive philosophy" of this world—had failed him, just like it failed the doctor. When the "new creation" took over, people like the doctor took notice and wanted to know why. The "new" was infectious.

Which brings us to the big idea for this chapter. It's the one idea that, fully understood and truly believed, can change everything:

When you seek your identity in Jesus Christ and his gospel, you will find a deep, lasting satisfaction so infectious that others will want it too.

This is where it can get tricky, because the questions "who am I, and why do I exist?" are not easy to answer, are they? There are many reasons for that, but I think two require a mention—our cultural moment and what is commonly called "the Fall."

OUR CULTURAL MOMENT

First, the cultural upheaval of our times doesn't help. Men today are under a cloud of suspicion. Regrettably, entertainment, news, and social media have created "a great mass of common assumptions"[1] about who men are—mostly negative.

As a result, the male identity has taken a beating. But the vast majority of us get out of bed every day and try to do the right thing. Of course, some men do wicked things, and their sins have given rise to stereotypes about men. From sex-crazed exploiters of women, to deadbeat dads, to macho men incapable of expressing emotions, to shallow frat boys, to greedy politicians and businessmen, to lazy and irresponsible man-boys who refuse to grow up and who want to play video games all day—these pejorative assumptions about a small minority of men have been repeated millions of times. Often enough to become an "outlook." Christian author C. S. Lewis put it so well:

> Every age has its own outlook . . . All contemporary writers share to some extent the contemporary outlook—even those, like myself, who seem most opposed to it. Nothing strikes me more when I read the controversies of past ages than the fact that both sides were usually assuming without question a good deal which we should now absolutely deny. They

thought that they were as completely opposed as two sides could be, but in fact they were all the time secretly united— united *with* each other and *against* earlier and later ages—by a great mass of common assumptions.[2]

You can fully become the man God created you to be. God's promise to you is that you don't have to be caged in "the contemporary outlook." Jesus Christ has come to set you free: "It is for freedom that Christ has set us free. Stand firm, then, and do not let yourselves be burdened again by a yoke of slavery" (Galatians 5:1). Jesus has provided a way of escape, which we'll explore in this book.

THE FALL

Second, we must manage our lives against the Fall. The Fall, described in Genesis 3, refers to the story of how sin and suffering pervasively entered the world through the sins of Adam and Eve. Because of the Fall, there are forces constantly trying to throw you into an identity crisis—the world, the flesh, and the devil.

I fully realize the mere suggestion of the Fall is one of the main reasons some men reject the Christian faith and worldview. But let me offer a few thoughts to reinforce our Christian conviction. Blaise Pascal wrote:

Without doubt nothing is more shocking to our reason than to say that the sin of the first man has implicated in its guilt men so far from the original sin that they seem incapable of sharing it. This flow of guilt does not seem merely impossible to us, but indeed most unjust . . . Certainly nothing jolts us more rudely than this doctrine, and

> yet, but for this mystery, the most incomprehensible of all,
> we remain incomprehensible to ourselves . . . Consequently
> it is not through the proud activity of our reason but through
> its simple submission that we can really know ourselves.[3]

The Fall is an offense to human reason, but once accepted, it makes perfect sense of the human condition. For example, the Fall explains why we must do our work while feeling the prick of thorns (Genesis 3:17–19). And it helps us understand why we sometimes have to enjoy the blazing beauty of a sunrise through thick glasses that grace the bridge of a runny nose.

Fortunately, the Bible makes a great pair of glasses for correcting our outlook. Just as we're warned to take precautions against cyber-hacking, consider these scriptural warnings about getting hacked by the world, flesh, or devil.

By the world. The apostle John wrote, "Do not love the world or anything in the world. If anyone loves the world, love for the Father is not in them. For everything in the world—the lust of the flesh, the lust of the eyes, and the pride of life—comes not from the Father but from the world. The world and its desires pass away, but whoever does the will of God lives forever" (1 John 2:15–17). The world includes all approaches to life, work, and family that conflict with Christianity, such as materialism and consumerism.

By the flesh. The flesh, on the other hand, refers to our own sinful natures. Jesus said, "What comes out of a person is what defiles them. For it is from within, out of a person's heart, that evil thoughts come—sexual immorality, theft, murder, adultery, greed, malice, deceit, lewdness, envy, slander, arrogance and folly. All these evils come from inside and defile a person" (Mark 7:20–23).

By the devil. The devil is the Hacker-in-Chief, intent on deceiving us, accusing us, and making us feel false condemnation, shame, and guilt. Jesus describes the devil this way: "He was a murderer from the beginning, not holding to the truth, for there is no truth in him. When he lies, he speaks his native language, for he is a liar and the father of lies" (John 8:44).

The devil wants nothing more than to rob you of your identity and make your life miserable, which led the apostle Peter to caution, "Be alert and of sober mind. Your enemy the devil prowls around like a roaring lion looking for someone to devour" (1 Peter 5:8).

Now it's time to clarify what we mean by "identity" so we know we're talking about the same thing.

YOUR "OBITUARY" IDENTITY

When you see yourself, who do you see? What pictures come to mind? Is it one of your *roles*—like husband or father? Is it *what you do*—your work or ministry? Is it a picture of *what you have*—like your home, money, and car? Is it *what you look like*—your appearance, your physique, or the color of your skin? Is it *who you know*—your relationships, acquaintances, or friends? Are you defined by *where you're from* or *who your family is*? Or do you see the kind of person you are in *character* and *conduct*? And how closely do you think the man you see compares to the man God sees?

Part of your identity is like the clothes you wear—what you do, what you have, what you look like, who you know, and where you live. These make up your "obituary" identity—the visible things others remember about you when you're gone.

Here's the problem: If what you do is who you are, then who are you when you don't do what you do anymore? If what you have, who you know, and where you're from is who you are, then who are you when those things go away? If they go away, does that mean your identity is lost?

YOUR "NAKED BEFORE GOD" IDENTITY

The other part of your identity is like the body under the clothes: what men say really matters most when they take stock of their lives—your wife, your children, your friends, your faith, your heart, your calling, your character, and how you conduct yourself. These make up your "naked before God" identity.

When David was picked to be the king of Israel, the Lord sent Samuel to the home of Jesse. When Samuel arrived, he saw Jesse's handsome oldest son and was ready to offer him the job. But the Lord said, "No, not him."

> But the LORD said to Samuel, "Do not consider his appearance or his height, for I have rejected him. The LORD does not look at the things people look at. *People look at the outward appearance, but the* LORD *looks at the heart."*
> *1 Samuel 16:7, emphasis added*

People will judge you by your appearance. God makes no such judgments. Who you are in your heart is who you really are. It's this "naked before God" identity that is our subject at hand.

Would you do me a favor? Would you take both your hands and, as much as possible, wrap them around your head? Now, for a few seconds, close your eyes and think about the stars and the enormity of space. Next, consider how small the head in your hands is in comparison—your consciousness, your intellect, your will, your emotions—everything the Bible calls the "heart." Who is this "man," and why do you exist?

It's humbling, isn't it?

Now imagine King David, the man after God's own heart, holding his head in his hands. He too asked that ultimate question about our identity—who are we, and why do we exist?

His answer, echoed throughout Scripture, gives us the Christian answer to who we are and what our lives are all about:

> When I consider your heavens,
>> the work of your fingers,
> the moon and the stars,
>> which you have set in place,
> *what is mankind that you are mindful of them,*
>> *human beings that you care for them?*

Our Identity—Who We Are

> *You have made them a little lower than the angels*
>> *and crowned them with glory and honor.*

Our Purpose—What Our Lives Are About

> *You made them rulers over the works of your hands;*
>> *you put everything under their feet.*
>>> *Psalm 8:3–6, headings and emphasis added*

When God looks at you, he doesn't just see you; he sees *himself*. We were made to *mirror* his identity. Theologians call this the *imago dei*—the image of God. Echoing Psalm 8:

> Then God said, *"Let us make mankind in our image, in our likeness,* so that they may rule over the fish in the sea and the birds in the sky, over the livestock and all the wild animals, and over all the creatures that move along the ground."

> *So God created mankind in his own image,*
>> *in the image of God he created them;*
>> *male and female he created them.*
>>> *Genesis 1:26–27, emphasis added*

Our identity—who we are, our "being," is like the angels and mirrors the image of God himself—repeated four times in the italicized parts of the verse above!

Why we exist—what our lives are all about, our "doing," is to tend the culture and build his kingdom. Basically, Jesus has said, "You're in charge until I get back."

Discovering who he was and what his life was all about is what made my friend Ken so infectious. And there's no reason we can't be just as infectious as he was. But where do we start? Perhaps the best place is to intentionally settle on the "roles" that are precious to us and the "attributes" we want to exhibit.

Identity as "Roles"

When I think of who I am and what my life is about, I primarily think about my roles. As I start each day, I pray along these lines:

> *Father, we come to meet and abide with you, our much-loved Creator, Sustainer, and Redeemer. We pray that you will meet and abide with us, your much-loved sons and daughters.*
>
> *Jesus, we come to meet and abide with you, our much-loved Savior, Lord, and Teacher. We pray that you will meet and abide with us, your much-loved disciples, friends, and servants.*
>
> *Holy Spirit, we come to meet and abide with you, our much-loved Comforter, Counselor, and Power. We pray that you will meet and abide with us, your much-loved temples, vessels, and charges.*

Let me pull out and list the roles I mention in my daily prayer:

Sons and daughters: Is there any greater joy than to "feel" completely loved and accepted without reservation?

Disciples: To be a disciple is the highest honor to which a man can aspire. We'll dive into this in much more detail later, but for now, let's define a disciple as someone who believes in Jesus and wants to model their life after his teachings and example.

Friends: In John 15:15, Jesus says, "I have called you friends, for everything that I learned from my Father I have made known to you."

Servants: Because of the love, grace, and mercy of Jesus, we feel like we can no longer be happy unless we serve him as an expression of our deep gratitude.

Temples: The Holy Spirit lives inside us. We "house" the presence of God. I think about that all the time.

Vessels: When we draw close to God, the Holy Spirit fills us with so much love, grace, mercy, kindness, and generosity that we have not only enough for ourselves but also an "overflow" that, like Ken, we can share with others through love and acts of service.

Charges: In John 14:26, the Holy Spirit has been charged to teach us all things and remind us of everything Jesus told us.

This, of course, is not an exhaustive list, but these are the roles precious to me. You can no doubt add other roles precious to you and delete some of mine. For example, you could add husband or steward.

The point, however, is that keeping such a list, whether written or mental, is a precise and excellent way to understand and constantly reinforce our identity. How would you describe your identity in terms of roles? Feel free to adopt or adapt my list. I suggest you write down these roles, which you can do right here:

- Husband, father, grandfather
- provider - family
- want to help others
- wanting to know more about the Bible
- how to help others coming closer to Christ live the life God wants me to

be a person wanting to pray for others - I ever thought prayer was not necessary or would I was so wrong

Identity as "Attributes"

Another way I think of who I am and what my life is about is the kind of man I want to be in *character* and *conduct*—or "attributes." God has not left this to chance. He has told us which attributes to prize most, and he has promised to give us those attributes freely through his Spirit out of the overflow of abiding in Christ:

> But the fruit of the Spirit is love, joy, peace, patience, kindness, goodness, faithfulness, gentleness, self-control.
>
> *Galatians 5:22–23 ESV*

And because it drips off nearly every page of the Bible, I think it's appropriate to add humility to any list of desirable identity attributes:

> God opposes the proud
>> but shows favor to the humble.
>
> *James 4:6*

Here are the attributes in list form:

- love
- joy
- peace
- patience
- kindness
- goodness
- faithfulness
- gentleness
- self-control
- humility

Does this list do justice to the identity attributes you would like to exhibit? If so, consider memorizing the two verses above so you will always have them on the tip of your tongue.

Remember, the fruit of the Spirit is what God does for you,

not what you do for God. One day, my friend Eric called and asked, "Pat, please pray for me to have patience." I explained he didn't need me to pray for his patience. He simply needed to walk in the power of the Holy Spirit, and patience would be the by-product. That's a much less painful way to get patience! The same can be said for all these attributes. They are not something we self-will into existence, but as Ken said about peace and joy, they are the fruit of walking with Jesus in the power of his Spirit.

A HUG AND A DECLARATION

How shall we tie off this chapter, because obviously tens of thousands of books have been written on the subject of identity? Let's go with these two ideas—a hug (something God can do for you) and a declaration (something you can do for God).

"Can I Give You a Hug?"—God

I've watched great speakers try to inspire men to go change the world by making appeals to their courage, pride, inner strength, moral obligation, sense of duty, willingness to make a sacrifice, and "this is what you really need to do." Those appeals, especially when emotionally charged, can get men amped up, jacked up, and fired up. For a while. But in most cases, the parted seas return to calm a few days later. The "new" has become "old" again, and men go back to their former way of life.

There is one thing, though, that I've seen really and truly change men's hearts. That is to bring men into the real presence of Jesus, even if only for a brief moment, to get a little larger glimpse of the God who is. What changes men's hearts is when they *feel* in their emotions what they *believe* in their minds—that

God really loves them without reservation, unconditionally, just as they are.

The calling I received from the Lord to leave business for full-time ministry is, "I want you to take my message of love to a broken generation." Because of that, I think God wants me to tell you he loves you very much. In fact, I think he wants to give you a hug. Listen carefully to what God has to say to you:

> I love you very much. I know your name. I knit you together in your mother's womb. All the days of your life were ordained before one of them came to pass. I have determined the exact times and places where you should live. Your times are in my hands. I know every thought you have from afar. I know every word you speak before it forms on the tip of your tongue. You are my new creation. You are the full expression of my creative genius. I was at my very best when I made you.

> I will never forsake or leave you. No one will be able to snatch you out of my hands. I began a good work in you and will carry it on to completion. When you are a battered reed, I will not break you off. When you are a smoldering wick, I will not put you out. Two sparrows are bought and sold for a penny, yet not one of them falls to the ground without my knowing it—and you are worth more than many sparrows. I am patient, not wanting anyone to perish. My word that goes out from my mouth to you will accomplish all this and achieve what I want.

The words in this "hug" are adapted straight from God's Word. I've purposely left out the references because I just want you to be able to read and absorb the tenderness of God's love for you. How do we respond to such wonderful news?

A Call to Action: Something You Can Do for God

Let's end this first chapter with a "call to action" and give you an opportunity to declare your identity "in Christ" and what your life is all about. By making the following declaration, you can affirm, "The old has gone, the new is here!"

MY DECLARATION OF CHRISTIAN MANHOOD

Heavenly Father, I am tired of weak, unsatisfying faith. I am weary of leading a divided life. I want to be so fully "in Christ" that others want to catch what I have. As a "new creation," I long to know your love for me as a son, disciple, friend, servant, temple, vessel, and charge of the Holy Spirit. I want to experience and infectiously exhibit all the fruit of your Spirit, with all humility.

So here today, I take my stand. I repent of all my worldly and sinful ways and put my faith in Christ alone. I hereby declare that from this day forward, I will stop seeking the God, or gods, I have wanted and will start seeking the God who is. I pledge to lead a Bible-saturated life of devotion and study of God.

My desire is to renew my mind, to be a man after God's own heart, to live out of the overflow of a vibrant relationship with Jesus, and to fully follow Jesus Christ with my whole heart each and every day. I will make it my business to live in right relationship with God and in right relationship with all people, and to exercise my gifts to fulfill your calling on my life.

My true identity is "in Christ." I commit to live openly for the glory of God in all my ways. I openly confess that I can do none of this apart from your grace, Father, through Jesus and the power of the Holy Spirit. Therefore, I pledge my allegiance this day to a life of Christ-centered manhood. If they cut me, I want to bleed Jesus. Amen.

_____ 5/11/22 _____ (sign and date)

Congratulations for taking a stand on your identity. Who you are in Christ is who you really are. In the next chapter, we'll explore how this understanding of our identity can transform our daily lives. But first consider these questions.

Reflection and Small Group Discussion Questions

1. Are you more like Ken or more like the doctor, or somewhere in between? If you had to write down your "naked before God" identity right now, what would it say?

2. In this chapter, we looked at identity in terms of our roles and attributes. Which of your roles are most important to you, and why? Which attributes do you most want to exhibit, and why? How does this approach help you better understand who you are and what your life is about?

3. Did you like the "hug from God"? Whether it's to embrace him for the first time or to reaffirm that you're a "new creation" in Christ, pray My Declaration of Christian Manhood (together if in a group) out loud as your closing prayer.

TWO

LIFE BALANCE

How to Be Faithful with Everything Entrusted to Me

Now it is required that those who have
been given a trust must prove faithful.

1 CORINTHIANS 4:2

You have all the time you need to do
everything God wants you to do.

For several weeks, James didn't return any of the six text messages I sent. When we finally connected, I just had to ask, "Why didn't you return any of my texts?"

He said, "Pat, I'm really sorry. I've had to work out of town for ten of the last thirty days. My wife isn't happy about all the travel. I missed our son's Little League championship game—he hit a double and drove in the winning run. My daughter is being bullied on social media, so that's taking an emotional toll. I have more than a hundred work-related emails, texts, and phone calls I still need to return. To be honest, I've just been so overwhelmed that I've felt paralyzed."

I get it, and I'm sure you do too. It's easy to get out of whack and not know how to fix it. The twenty-four men who set the contents for this book were only one vote shy of making life balance their #1 issue, asking questions like:

- What should a typical day look like for a Christian man?
- How do I balance everyday life without losing focus on God and what's important?
- How do I prioritize effectively?
- In what ways can I get out of my normal routine and create a godly one?
- What are some applicable tips to help me use my time better, especially for personal growth?
- I want everything I do to reflect Jesus. I want integration there. I want a clean break between my work and my family. How do I do that?
- Are hobbies okay?

These are the questions of men who understand they've been given a trust—something to steward and take care of. They *want* to be found faithful.

As we've already said, no man fails on purpose. But most of us have more demands on our time than we have time to give—money pressures, work pressures, marriage pressures, parenting pressures, social pressures, health pressures. All kinds of pressures! And these pressures mount up.

So how do we solve this problem? How can you juggle all the demands on your time, intellect, emotions, money, and relationships? What is the healthy mix?

JESUS AND THE PRESSURES OF LIFE

The Bible teaches that Jesus was both fully God and fully human—a great mystery! *Human* Jesus had the same problem as we do—he couldn't be in more than one place at a time. Like us, he was constantly pulled in too many directions. Like us, he felt the pressures that can lead to an unbalanced life.

Jesus was once up most of the night healing people in Capernaum (Luke 4:31–41), where his ministry was headquartered. The Scripture reads, "At daybreak, Jesus went out to a solitary place. The people were looking for him and when they came to where he was, they tried to keep him from leaving them" (Luke 4:42).

Why did they try to keep Jesus from leaving? The better you are at what you do, the more people will want from you. That's just human nature. But it will always feel like pressure. How did Jesus handle the pressure? "But he said, 'I must proclaim the good news of the kingdom of God to the other towns also, because that is why I was sent'" (Luke 4:43).

Jesus knew who he was and what his life was all about—his identity. As a result, he had settled in his mind what God wanted to accomplish through him. How did Jesus solve the "too much to do" problem? He was intentional. He took control of his calendar: "And he kept on preaching in the synagogues of Judea" (Luke 4:44).

We are Christians today because Jesus "kept on preaching." Because Jesus lived by his priorities (not his pressures), he had all the time he needed to do everything God wanted him to do. You can too.

And that brings us to the big idea for this chapter: you have all the time you need to do everything God wants you to do. In this chapter, I'm going to help you settle in your mind what God wants to accomplish through you and for you. By the end, you will

- understand what priorities are and how they get set
- decide on and rank your own priorities
- complete a *specific-to-you* plan to help you be intentional, control your calendar, and live a more balanced life

WHAT ARE PRIORITIES?

A priority is anything to which you assign a high degree of urgency or importance. Priorities are what we decide in advance that matters most. As such, they precede goal setting and decision making. Priorities help us manage the pressures that will otherwise manage us.

Priorities can be daily, short-term, or long-term. For our purposes we're focused on the long-term priorities that will keep us balanced, such as loving God, staying married, being a

good dad, doing work that matters, and maintaining financial
security.

The key, as with Jesus, is to decide our priorities *in advance*.
Priorities are like downloading a preplanned hike into your GPS
app so you'll always be able to tell if you're where you wanted
to be. Once you lock down your priorities, for all intents and
purposes you're literally writing *future* history.

HOW MANY PRIORITIES CAN ONE MAN JUGGLE?

Having too many priorities is a common complaint. A *Harvard
Business Review* article cited a study of 1,800 global executives in
which two-thirds of them said they had too many conflicting priorities.[1] If you've ever worked at a company or business like that,
you and your coworkers probably felt like the business strategy
was incoherent.

Investor Warren Buffet, the "Oracle of Omaha," said you can
only handle five priorities. He was fanatical about knowing what
you want, learning the tools you needed to get there, whittling
your list of priorities down to five, and then making everything
beyond your top five priorities what he called your "avoid at all
cost" list.[2]

Of course, there's no iron law about how many priorities a
man can have. We are much too diverse for that. And priorities
change with the seasons of life. Nevertheless, in the commonsense
world, we know that men who can focus on doing a few things
well tend to get a better result than men who don't. The odds of
success go down each time you add something new. That's why we
have the saying, "He was a jack of all trades but master of none."
There are only so many hours in a day.

WHAT ARE THE PRIORITIES OF THE CHRISTIAN MAN?

There's no cookie-cutter description of "the Christian man." Priorities are not "one size fits all." A follower of Jesus in Pakistan will have a vastly different mental picture of a "win" than a middle-class American. That said, we all share approximately the same priorities.

While there's no universal map that will get you to your destination, the following five biblical priorities will help you manage those pressures that will otherwise manage you. As the saying goes, "If you don't know where you're going, then any road will get you there."

Reflect on how each of the following aligns with where you are today and where you would like to be in ten years. Later, you'll have an opportunity to use those reflections in a self-assessment. Also, once you've read these over, I suggest you take a personal retreat to adjust or change your priorities and to fill in the blank spaces provided below with your personal goals. I've added some "retreat verses" for further reflection. Your retreat could last for an hour or a half day, or you could go to a cabin and spend the night.

1. Loving God

Notwithstanding everything just said, loving God is the unequivocal top priority for the Christian man. When Jesus was asked, "Teacher, which is the greatest commandment in the Law?" he replied, "'Love the Lord your God with all your heart and with all your soul and with all your mind.' This is the first and greatest commandment" (Matthew 22:36–38).

The word *first* in the verse comes from the Greek word *protos*, from which we get words like *prototype* ("first of a kind"). The word *greatest* comes from the Greek word *megas*, from which we get the words that start with *mega*. Loving God is the proto-mega-commandment.

Loving God is what matters most. We are to love God with the totality of our being, every ounce of our energy, and the sum of our strength. Saint Augustine said, "Love, and do what thou wilt," which others have paraphrased, "Love God, and do what you want."[3]

Of course, the Bible doesn't say that specifically—it's hyperbole. However, Jesus did say, "If you love me, keep my commands . . . Whoever has my commands and keeps them is the one who loves me . . . Anyone who loves me will obey my teaching" (John 14:15, 21, 23).

So while Augustine and the paraphrasers were speaking in hyperbole, there's also a strong argument that it makes really good theology. The more we love God, the more we want what he wants.

Here are five ways we can enhance our love for God.

Knowing God

The famous preacher and writer Charles Spurgeon reportedly said, "I do not believe there have been fifteen minutes of consecutive waking time in forty years when I have not been distinctly conscious of the presence of our blessed Lord."[4]

There is a God we want, and there is a God who is. They are not the same God. One day it hit me: wishing for "the God I want" won't have one iota of impact on God's unchanging nature. The turning point of our lives is when we stop seeking the God we want and start seeking the God who is.

Our job is not to change God, but rather to let him change the core affections of our hearts. That happens when we humbly make Jesus the Lord of our lives, not just our Savior. To make Jesus Lord means to bring our entire lives under his authority.

Retreat verses: Psalm 96:1–9; Ezekiel 1:25–28; Revelation 4, 5, 21, 22.

Sample Goal: I really want to get to know Jesus. I will search for the God of the Bible, inviting him to change the core affections of my heart. I will begin each day with faith and repentance. I will make Jesus the Lord of my life.

My Goal: _____

_____

_____

*As you read along, consider jotting down a personal goal in the spaces provided, even if it's just a first draft.

Self-Examination

Christian writer Richard Foster said, "Superficiality is the curse of our age . . . The desperate need today is not for a greater number of intelligent people, or gifted people, but for deep people."[5]

We live in a wonderful age, but it has a dark side. Many of us today are in a structural hurry—a fast pace is structured into our lives. The price of this pace is peace. Resolve to periodically call a time-out to peer into your soul. John Calvin famously wrote, "Nearly all the wisdom we possess . . . consists of two parts: the knowledge of God and of ourselves."[6]

Retreat verses: Psalms 17:3; 26:1–12; 32:8; 139:1–24; 2 Corinthians 10:3–5; 13:5.

Sample Goal: I will calendarize two hours on the first Saturday morning of each month to slow down, examine my heart, think deeply about my life, and make needed changes based on how I understand God's larger purposes for my life.

My Goal: _____

_____

_____

The Bible

Personally, I have never known a man whose life has changed in any significant way apart from the regular study of God's Word. Most of us have heard someone say, "I knew about God, but I didn't know God." Perhaps a greater problem today is that people do know God, but they don't know about him.

The single best way to know God is to personally read his bestselling book—the Bible. We don't use our personal experience to interpret our Bibles; we use our Bibles to interpret our personal experience. I don't just read my Bible; my Bible reads me.

Retreat verses: Psalms 1:1–3; 119:9–11; 89–104; John 20:30–31; Romans 15:4; 2 Timothy 3:16–17

Sample Goal: This year, I am going to read through *The One Year Bible* and memorize one Scripture verse each month.

My Goal: _____

_____

_____

Prayer

Martin Luther is reported to have famously said, "I have so much business I cannot get on without spending three hours daily in prayer."[7]

A man interviewing for a position with our ministry asked, "Are you a praying ministry?" His interviewer answered, "Yes." Then he said, "Just so there is no misunderstanding, I'm not just asking if you believe in prayer, but do you pray?"

Let's not just believe in prayer—let's pray! Prayer is the currency of our personal relationship with Jesus.

Pray throughout the day, because praying once a day is like eating one potato chip. Prayer is meant to be a constant conversation with a Father who wants to give you everything you need. Prayer is hard work, but it releases the power of God into human actions.

Retreat verses: Matthew 6:5–15; Ephesians 6:18; 1 Thessalonians 5:17; James 5:16

Sample Goal: I will spend time in prayer before making any major decision. I will begin each day with prayer.

My Goal: _____

_____

_____

Church

The Bible does not say, "Your enemy the devil prowls around like a roaring lion looking for some group to devour." It says he is looking for "someone"—one person—"to devour" (1 Peter 5:8). A wily wolf doesn't attack the flock; he waits for a lone sheep to stray away.

Here is a great irony: generally, the least involved people in church are the ones who need it most. Yet the church often ministers best to its most involved members. The solution? If you are a needy person, get more involved (although I understand that's not an easy ask if you're hurting, especially when it's the church that has hurt your feelings).

What if you're already actively engaged in your church? Spend time reaching out to people on the fringe of your church. They're easy to spot. They're the unengaged ones who act like everything's okay, so that's why they're not more engaged. I can assure you—they're not okay.

Retreat verses: Hebrews 10:23–25; 1 Peter 5:8.

Sample Goal: I will seek ways to be actively involved in both becoming a disciple and making disciples through my church.

My Goal: _____

_____

_____

We will do a deeper dive into loving God in the next chapter: "Growth: Becoming a More Kingdom-Minded Man."

I hope you will find these different ways to love God helpful as you pursue a more balanced life. Now let's turn to the second of five priorities for the Christian man.

2. Loving People

Cut the Bible, and it bleeds neighbor love. After Jesus replied that the first and greatest commandment is loving God, he continued, "And the second is like it: 'Love your neighbor as yourself.' All the Law and the Prophets hang on these two commandments" (Matthew 22:39–40).

Jesus did not leave our two top priorities open to interpretation! He even upped the ante in the book of John to *as I have loved you*: "*A new command* I give you: Love one another. *As I have loved you*, so you must love one another" (John 13:34, emphasis added).

The priority of loving people captures *the essence of everything* taught in both the Old and New Testaments. Does that sound like overstatement? See for yourself:

> Let no debt remain outstanding, except the continuing debt to love one another, for whoever loves others has fulfilled the law. The commandments, "You shall not commit adultery," "You shall not murder," "You shall not steal," "You shall not covet," and whatever other command there may be, are summed up in this one command: "Love your neighbor as yourself." Love does no harm to a neighbor. Therefore love is the *fulfillment* of the law.
>
> *Romans 13:8–10, emphasis added*

> So in *everything*, do to others what you would have them do to you, for this *sums up* the Law and the Prophets.
>
> *Matthew 7:12, emphasis added*

For the entire law is *fulfilled* in keeping this one command:
"Love your neighbor as yourself."

Galatians 5:14, emphasis added

Love is the glue that can hold us together and the oil that can
keep us from rubbing each other the wrong way. So "above all,
love each other deeply, because love covers over a multitude of
sins" (1 Peter 4:8).

Let's explore the places where we want love and talk about
how to share it.

Loving My Wife (If Married)

Most men are either married or hope to be one day. If we
take all the problems of men and put the marriage problem in
one stack and the other problems in another stack, the marriage
problem alone is still higher than all the other problems combined.
Easily the number one problem most men face today is that their
marriages are not working the way God intended. When the party
is over, the lights are dimmed, and the kids are grown and gone,
there will only be two rocking chairs sitting side by side. You and
your wife really are the only two who are in this thing together.

Retreat verses: 1 Corinthians 7:1–17; Ephesians 5:25–31;
1 Peter 3:7

Sample Goal: I will prove by the way I spend my time that
my wife is truly the most important person in my life after God
but before all others.

My Goal: _____

_____

_____

We will do a deeper dive into marriage in chapter 4: "Marriage: Finding a New Best Friend in My Wife."

Loving My Children (If a Father)

If your children are doing well, all of your other problems will fit into a thimble. No amount of success at work can adequately compensate for failure at home. So be your children's spiritual leader, greatest fan, encourager, cheerleader, champion, mentor, and example. Pray for them. Spend time with them in ways they want to receive it—board games, outings, watching their sporting events . . . Tell each child every day, "I love you!" and "I'm proud of you!"—like God told his Son in Matthew 3:17.

Retreat verses: Deuteronomy 11:18–21; Psalm 78:1–8; Ephesians 6:4; Colossians 3:23.

Sample Goal: I will rotate taking one child each week on a "fun date," tell each child I love them and I'm proud of them every day, and pray for them each day.

My Goal: _____

_____

_____

We will do a deeper dive into fathering in chapter 5: "Children: A Dad Who Really Makes a Difference."

Authentic Friendships

Mother Teresa once reflected on what she saw as the greatest problem facing the world. In her book *A Simple Path*, she wrote, "The greatest disease in the West today is not TB or leprosy; it is being unwanted, unloved, uncared for. We can cure physical diseases with medicine, but the only cure for loneliness, despair and hopelessness is love."[8]

Most of us could name our six pallbearers, but do you have a friend you can call at 2:00 a.m.? You will be fortunate in life if you have three real friends. Friendship is hard work. It takes time to build trust. Accountability—a step deeper—means giving a few people permission to ask you how you are *really* doing. Nothing will do more to keep you on track.

Retreat verses: Proverbs 27:6, 17; Ecclesiastes 4:9–10; John 13:34; Galatians 6:1–2; Philippians 2:4

Sample Goal: This year, I will either start or join a weekly men's small group (or become even more committed to the group I'm already in).

My Goal: _____

_____

_____

We will do a deeper dive into friendship in chapter 6: "Friendships: Finding and Keeping Godly Friends."

Next let's introduce the third of our five priorities.

3. Vocation

Vocation, in the spiritual sense, is a divine summons to serve God. That includes work, of course, but I've also included the ways we support good health so we don't get burned out.

Work

You don't have to work seventy hours a week to be successful. In fact, if you work that much, you can be pretty sure you're failing everywhere else.

Most people will spend more time at work than any other place. Work is not merely a platform to do ministry; it *is* ministry. Our work is a holy vocation. Do your work with uncompromising excellence, as if doing it for the Lord Jesus—because you are! (see Colossians 3:23). And as the theologian-philosopher Francis Schaeffer reportedly said, "If you do your work well, you will have a chance to speak."

Retreat verses: Genesis 1:27–28; 2:4–15; 3:17–19; Colossians 3:22–24.

Sample Goal: I will stop thinking of work as merely a means to other ends and begin to look for intrinsic value in the work I do. My life's work is "serving others."

My Goal: _____

_____

_____

We will do a deeper dive into work in chapter 7: "Work: How Should I Think about My Work?"

Health, Leisure, Rest, Recreation

Jesus didn't say, "Come to me, all you who are weary and burdened, *and I will give you more work to do!*" He said, "Come to me . . . and I will give you rest" (Matthew 11:28). If we don't take care of ourselves, it's often because we don't think we have time. But with God, you have all the time you need to do all the things God wants you to do.

No one else can take responsibility for our private lives. Health includes mental, emotional, physical, and spiritual wholeness. Health is a gift from God, but we are responsible to create a proper balance with rest, recreation, nutrition, and exercise.

For example, since I sit in front of a computer a lot, I like to practice "temple maintenance" by averaging about one hour a day of physical activity. Keep a sabbath—one day a week set aside for worship, rest, relaxation, and spending time with those you care about the most. Even Chick-fil-A does this. Did you know that a Chick-fil-A makes more money in six days than a McDonald's makes in seven?

Retreat verses: Matthew 6:25–34; 11:28; 1 Corinthians 3:16–17; 1 Timothy 4:8

Sample Goal: This year, I will study one new subject completely foreign to my normal routines (e.g., astronomy, interior design, sailing), read a book for pleasure, and exercise three times each week. I will get off Adderall.

My Goal: _____

_____

_____

Next is our fourth priority.

4. Money

There's no pressure like cash flow pressure. It's hard to keep your chin up when you can't pay your bills.

Money, and how to handle it, *needs* to be a priority—which probably explains why Jesus talked so much about money and the things it can buy. Howard Dayton, one of the world's leading experts on what the Bible teaches about finance, said, "The Bible contains 2,350 verses dealing with money and possessions, and 15 percent of everything Jesus said had to do with it."[9] The Bible can correct the error that most men think money will do what it won't, and that God won't do what he will. Pray for a "conversion of the wallet." Be generous. Be a steward. Develop a financial plan that leads to financial security. As Solomon tells us, "The wise store up choice food and olive oil" (Proverbs 21:20).

Retreat verses: Matthew 6:24; 2 Corinthians 8–9; 1 Timothy 6:6–10.

Sample Goal: This year I will tithe 10 percent by faith and save 5 percent. I will meet with a financial planner.

My Goal: _____

_____

_____

Let's conclude with a preliminary look at our fifth priority.

5. Ministry

Brother Lawrence was a humble seventeenth-century Carmelite lay brother who worked in a monastery kitchen and repaired shoes. In *The Practice of the Presence of God*, he wrote, "I tell you that this sweet and loving gaze of God insensibly kindles a divine fire in the soul which is set ablaze so ardently with the love of God that one is obliged to perform exterior acts to moderate it."[10] Dwight L. Moody, perhaps the greatest evangelist of the nineteenth century, said, "The reward of service is more service."[11] Bob Dylan sang, "Well, it may be the devil or it may be the Lord, but you're gonna have to serve somebody."[12] And Jesus prayed to the Father, "As you sent me into the world, I have sent them into the world" (John 17:18).

We are sent to live for Christ. *Service is its own reward*. We belong to Jesus. Use your spiritual gift(s) for the glory of God by loving and serving others. I'm praying in faith that your life will make a difference—in your calling as a spouse, parent, provider, churchman, witness, servant, and friend. Discover your "spiritual gifts" (more on this in the next chapter on Growth). Everything we do can be ministry.

Retreat verses: Matthew 28:18–20; 2 Timothy 2:2; 1 Peter 4:8–11

Sample Goal: This year I will gain a better understanding of my spiritual gifting and ask my pastor for a way to use it.

My Goal: _____

_____

_____

I'll give you a guide to discover your spiritual gifts in the next chapter. We will also do a deeper dive into ministry in chapter 10: "Sharing My Faith: Having Authentic Spiritual Conversations with My Friends."

A PERSONAL SELF-ASSESSMENT

In a parable told by Jesus, a man entrusted bags of gold to three men. After a long time, the man came to settle accounts. Two of the men had been faithful stewards with their "trust" funds. They both heard, "Well done, good and faithful servant! You have been faithful with a few things; I will put you in charge of many things. Come and share your master's happiness!" (Matthew 25:21, 23).

Now that we've overviewed these five biblical priorities, take this self-audit to assess how much of a "faithful servant" you have been so far. Circle the answer that best describes how faithful you have been for each of the five priorities we've been discussing.

Then in the blank spaces, rank your priorities in their current order of importance from 1 to 5.

____**Loving God**
Very faithful | mostly faithful | somewhat faithful | not faithful
____**Loving Wife, Children, Friends**
Very faithful | mostly faithful | somewhat faithful | not faithful
____**Vocation: Work, Rest, Recreation, Health**
Very faithful | mostly faithful | somewhat faithful | not faithful
____**Money**
Very faithful | mostly faithful | somewhat faithful | not faithful
____**Ministry**
Very faithful | mostly faithful | somewhat faithful | not faithful

How did you do? Did you see something that surprised you? That would be normal. Management guru Peter Drucker noted that most executives say they spend their time one way, but when he asked them to keep a journal, they soon discovered they spent time much differently than they thought. That's why I asked you to write things down. As the sixteenth-century philosopher Francis Bacon said, "Reading maketh a full man . . . and writing an exact man."[13]

THE STARTING POINT TO ADJUST YOUR PRIORITIES

Let's assume you decide you'd like to adjust or change your priorities.

Here's the twist. Don't start by asking, "What do my priorities need to be?"

Instead, start by asking, "What do I want—really?"

I suggest this because we often say, "I need this. I need that. I ought to do this or the other." And then what do we do? We do what we want. For example, if you didn't take this approach, you might say, "I need to love God more," when what you really want is more of the riches and pleasures this life has to offer.

Why is this distinction so important? Early in my career, I discovered that people do what they want—even when I'm paying their salaries! For example, I interviewed John to manage our accounting department. He really needed a job and convinced me this was something he could do and wanted to do. But within a few weeks, it became clear John would rather do the accounting work himself than manage a team. It didn't work out. That's why during employment interviews, I now spend very little time explaining what we need the candidate to do. I spend most of my time trying to figure out what they want to do. Why? Because I know that regardless of what we need, once they get settled, they're going to gravitate toward what they want to do.

Let's say, for example, you keep it real and admit to yourself that loving God is not the thing you want most—not really. That's huge because now you can ask the right question.

What do I mean? If loving God isn't your top priority, it's a nonstarter to ask, "What do I need to do to love God more?"

Asking that question will lead you to answers like, "I need to read my Bible more, have a regular quiet time, attend church more regularly, join a weekly men's Bible study, serve on a church committee, etc." That's a performance-based approach that doesn't get at what's really going on in your heart.

The right question is, "Okay, if this priority (e.g., loving God) is not what I really want, how do I change?"

You can pray, "Lord, I have not been faithful with this or that priority. I have not been faithful because what I have really wanted is this other thing. I openly confess I have had my priorities mixed up—that I have not wanted to _____ [say, love God]. But I *want* to want it."

God can work with that. His Spirit is already in you, waiting to release his power on every problem you face. All you have to do is ask. He will change the core affections of your heart.

Here's the irony. You may end up taking the same actions as in the performance-based approach (e.g., have regular quiet time, attend church more often), but your motivation will be entirely different.

If this concept is new to you, I suggest you reread this section until you can make it your own.

SQUEEZING OUT ENOUGH TIME

Possibly the biggest obstacle to living a balanced life is squeezing out enough time. No man can do everything. Choices must be made.

Here's a practical tip to invest your limited time and money where they count the most: *Don't give yourself to those who don't absolutely need you at the expense of those who do.* Triage is the military technique of deciding how to prioritize treatment of wounded soldiers when a wave of new casualties swamps the capacity of the medic unit. The helicopters bring back three groups of wounded soldiers:

- those who will live if they receive immediate treatment
- those who will live even if treatment is delayed
- those who will die no matter what is done

When arranged like that, the order of treatment becomes obvious. In a similar way, we can do a little civilian triage and arrive at an obvious way to prioritize when we're faced with competing time demands:

- those who can't live without you, or you without them
- those you would help if you don't have to neglect group #1
- those who will be fine with or without you

As I wrote in *The Man in the Mirror*, prioritize everything you do on the basis of who's going to be crying at your funeral.

GETTING THE RIGHT THINGS DONE

Of course, long-term priorities have to be reflected in how we prioritize on a daily basis.

At the very beginning of my career I heard an idea that I've used ever since. The way I heard the story is that in 1918, Charles M. Schwab, the president of Bethlehem Steel, was concerned about inefficiency at his company. He hired a business consultant named Ivy Lee, who coached all the executives to write down their top priorities for the day—no more than ten things. Then Lee told them, "Start on #1 and don't get distracted until you finish. Then move on to #2 and execute it completely without distraction. Then go on to #3, #4, and so on."

Lee said, "If you don't finish your list, don't worry about it. Say you only complete four items on your list. At least you will know you've done the four most important things. Then when you make your list for the following day, you can move today's unfinished items to the top of the list. In so doing, you will always be working on the highest priorities you have."

Schwab thought it was a silly idea. But Lee convinced him to give it a try and said, "Send me a check for whatever you think the idea is worth."

A few months later, Schwab sent Ivy Lee a check for $25,000 ($475,000 adjusted for inflation) and said it was the single greatest business idea he had ever received.

THE POWER OF A "SPECIFIC" ACTION PLAN

Winston wanted to reboot his previously successful real estate career, so he decided to make it a higher priority. Over several months, he poured a great deal of effort into a social media strategy, but it wasn't getting traction fast enough.

He reconnected with a former mentor who suggested social media was "speculative" marketing. His mentor advised, "You have a lot of highly satisfied previous clients. Sit down every day and phone ten former clients, tell them how much you appreciate their former business, and let them know you're looking for new business and to please let you know if they have any suggestions. Do that, and your business will take off again."

Winston said, "I'll do that." He started immediately. Every day he'd sit down and make those ten calls. Two weeks later, the floodgates opened. Business started coming in over the gunwales. He called his mentor. He said, "I don't get it. I'm doing what you said, and my business is rebooting and taking off. But very little of the business has come from any of the phone calls I've made!"

His mentor laughed. He said, "I never told you your business would take off from the phone calls you're making. I just said that if you faithfully made ten calls a day, your business would reboot and take off. Word gets around when you're open for business!"

When I told this story to my wife, I finished by saying, "That's the power of a plan!"

She added, "Yes, the power of a *specific* plan."

Winston was able to get something going by taking a few simple steps in the right direction. It's what psychologists technically call "behavioral activation" because it includes its own positive reinforcement and can snowball. Another example would be to say, "I'm going to walk to the end of the block," and then, "Oh, that was easy. Next time I can go for twenty minutes."

That's the power of priorities, and that's the power of a specific plan.

A CALL TO ACTION

The call to action for this chapter is to set aside two or three hours for a personal retreat and really drill down on what you want your priorities and goals to be. I hope you will accept that challenge! For now, here's a prayer you can pray to close this chapter:

Heavenly Father, thank you so much that you have not left us on our own to figure out how to be faithful with everything that has been entrusted to us. You've given us a road map in the Scriptures and lots of practical ideas as well so that we can be intentional. We pray, Father, that you would help each of us to be those faithful, reliable men. We pray that you'd help each of us take and apply these ideas to find your will, not merely to do what we want. Give us the desire and power to be found faithful. In Jesus' name, Amen.

Reflection and Small Group Discussion Questions

1. The big idea for this chapter is, "You have all the time you need to do everything God wants you to do." Do you feel like you have all the time you need, or are you stressed out? Explain your answer.

2. What did Jesus say our most important priorities are in Matthew 22:37–40? What did Augustine mean when he said, as paraphrased, "Love God, and do what you want?"

3. What have been your top three, four, or five priorities in life (what they really have been, not merely what you're supposed to say because you're a Christian)? What would you like your priorities to be in the future? Set aside some time to go through the five priorities in this chapter and write down a goal for each of the areas discussed. If possible, share your work with a small group of men who study the book together.

THREE

GROWTH

Becoming a More Kingdom-Minded Man

Do not conform to the pattern of this world,
but be transformed by the renewing of your mind.
Then you will be able to test and approve what
God's will is—his good, pleasing and perfect will.

PAUL TO THE ROMANS, ROMANS 12:2

A Bible, a small group, and
serving someone else will solve
90 percent of your problems.

On Friday mornings, I teach men at The Man in the Mirror Bible Study. After the message, the men sit around tables and discuss the topic of the day. While they unpack the lesson, I meet with our first-timers and spend a few minutes giving them the lay of the land.

Then I ask each visitor to take a few minutes to answer the question, "Where are you today on your spiritual journey?" Their answers roughly fall into three categories.

The first kind of man we might call a *seeker* or *inquirer*, a man who really doesn't know God yet in a personal way through his Son, Jesus, but who for whatever reason feels drawn to investigate the Christian faith.

The second kind of man we might call a *new Christian*, a man who recently made a profession of faith and now wants to figure out, "What did I just sign up for?"

The third kind of man let's call a *longtime Christian*, a man who has known God for a while—maybe several years—but is sensing a need to mobilize or remobilize:

- Maybe he was in a Bible study once but hasn't been in one for a while.
- Maybe he's looking for a place where he can build some friendships with like-minded men.
- Or perhaps he's a man who made a profession of faith at a younger age but has spent the last five, ten, fifteen, or more years living by his own ideas. His life has not turned out the way he planned. He has realized, or is beginning to realize, that he either needs to get to, or back to, a more biblical Christianity.

As different as they are, what all these men have in common is a deeply felt hunger to know more about God. In fact, spiritual growth was the number one issue cited by the twenty-four men who helped storyboard *The Christian Man*.

THE GOAL OF SPIRITUAL GROWTH

You've probably heard someone say, and maybe you've said it yourself, "I knew *about* God, but I didn't *know* God."

However, it's also true that a lot of men can say, and maybe you too, "I *know* God, but I don't know *about* God." Yes, there has been a profession of faith, but they feel like children stuck in elementary school. They believe the gospel—they know God. But they want—and need—to take the next step.

What is the next right step? When Jesus gave us his last or nearly last words, he uttered the single most impactful speech ever recorded in the history of the world. More millions of people and billions of dollars have been mobilized by this short speech than any other, and there isn't a close second:

> "All authority in heaven and on earth has been given to me.
> Therefore go and make disciples of all nations, baptizing
> them in the name of the Father and of the Son and of the
> Holy Spirit, and teaching them to obey everything I have
> commanded you. And surely I am with you always, to the
> very end of the age."
>
> *Matthew 28:18–20*

We call this well-known text the Great Commission. It's "great" because *becoming a disciple* is the "normal" way God has ordained to release the power of his gospel on your problems and opportunities.

The goal of spiritual growth, then, is to become a disciple. To become a disciple is the highest honor to which you can aspire.

This leads us to ask the question: What is a disciple, and how do you become one?

What Is a Disciple, and How Do You Become One?

The Greek word for disciple is *mathetes*, which literally translates "pupil" or "learner." When attached to Jesus, the term *disciple* has come to mean someone who follows and adheres to the person and teachings of Jesus.

Here's a biblical and actionable way to think about what it means to be a disciple. A disciple is:

- *called* to live "in" Christ (*knowing* God, salvation)
- *equipped* to live "like" Christ (knowing *about* God, spiritual growth)
- *sent* to live "for" Christ (living powerfully by the biblical priorities you set in chapter 2)

Let's elaborate on these three aspects.

Called to Live "In Christ"

In theology, "knowing God" pertains to the Greek word *kerygma*, which stands for "the proclamation of the gospel." It's knowing enough about the birth, life, death, and resurrection of Jesus to believe the good news through faith and repentance. The first step to become a disciple is to believe the *kerygma*. But as the writer of Hebrews noted, the call to live in Christ amounts to "elementary teachings":

Therefore let us move beyond the elementary teachings about Christ and be taken forward to maturity, not laying again the foundation of repentance from acts that lead to death, and of faith in God.

Hebrews 6:1

At some point on his journey, every Christian man wants to move beyond the elementary teachings. He feels a pang in his heart to grow in maturity, love, knowledge, wisdom, humility, and power. He wants to experience and exhibit all the fruit of the Holy Spirit—his love, joy, peace, patience, kindness, goodness, faithfulness, gentleness, and self-control (Galatians 5:22–23 ESV). He can no longer be happy only *knowing* God. He feels compelled to know *about* God too.

Equipped to Live "Like Christ"

The "knowing about God" part of theology pertains to the Greek word *didache*, or "the teachings." What many men are saying is, "I have put my faith in Christ. I *know* him. But now I want—no, I *need*—to know more *about* him. I want to grow into a more kingdom-minded man."

Men desperately need "the teachings." Not only do they tell us what we want to know about God, the teachings also give us wisdom and guidance for our marriages, families, friendships, work, sexuality, culture, and personal ministries—the seven issues that occupy the remaining chapters of this book—and for every other thing.

To be a Christian and *not* be discipled into "the teachings" is like a man joining the army and being issued a rifle that he never learns how to clean and shoot. He will not be of much use to himself or those around him on the day of battle.

Evangelism without discipleship is cruel.

Sent to Live "for Christ"

As a man eventually fills up to the overflow in his personal relationship with Jesus, he will come to a point when he feels he not only has enough Jesus for himself, but an "excess" that he can share with others. A spirit of gratitude suddenly compels him to do all the good things he has ever wanted to do but for which he previously lacked the power.

A young Dwight L. Moody, who became one of the most famous Christians of the late 1800s, was such a man. One day he heard, "The world has yet to see what God will do with and for and through and in and by the man who is fully and wholly consecrated to Him."

Moody thought to himself, "He said a man . . . he did not say a great man, nor a learned man, nor a rich man, nor a wise man, nor an eloquent man, nor a 'smart' man, but simply 'a man.' I am a man, and it lies with the man himself whether he will or will not make that entire and full consecration. I will try my utmost to be that man."[1]

Overwhelmed by his growing knowledge and experience of Christ's love, grace, and mercy (his discipleship), Moody felt compelled to live out to the ends of his fingertips for Jesus!

He became the hero of his story. And by making "that entire and full consecration," so can you. How does that happen? What are the steps?

SPIRITUAL DISCIPLINES: THE PORTAL TO SPIRITUAL GROWTH

Jesus wants to bring men—you, me, our sons, our families, everyone who is willing—to full maturity. It's the elephant in the narthex, which is why

Christ himself gave the apostles, the prophets, the evangelists, the pastors and teachers, *to **equip** his people for works
of service, so that the body of Christ may be built up* until we
all reach unity in the faith and *in the **knowledge** of the Son
of God and become mature, attaining to the whole measure of
the fullness of Christ* [*called* to live "in" Christ].

Then we will no longer be infants, tossed back and
forth by the waves, and blown here and there by every wind
of teaching and by the cunning and craftiness of people
in their deceitful scheming. Instead, speaking the truth
in love, *we will **grow** to become in every respect the mature
body of him who is the head, that is, Christ* [*equipped* to live
"like" Christ].

From him *the whole body, joined and held together by
every supporting ligament, grows and builds itself up in love, as
each part does its **work*** [*sent* to live "for" Christ].

*Ephesians 4:11–16, emphasis, bolding,
and bracketed comments added*

Much of the growth described in this regal thirty-thousand-
foot overview about how to make mature, fruitful disciples is
accomplished through *spiritual disciplines*.

Spiritual disciplines are simply the regular habits of men
(and women too, of course, but this is a men's book!) who
are being called, equipped, and sent to live in, like, and for
Jesus. In my book *A Man's Guide to the Spiritual Disciplines*,
I explained how God reveals himself in four types of spiritual
disciplines:[2]

- his *works* (in creation, or "general" revelation)
- his *Word* (in Scripture, or "special" revelation)

- the *"whisper"* of the Holy Spirit (prayer, worship, Sabbath, fellowship, counsel, fasting, and spiritual warfare)
- the *witness* of believers (stewardship, service, and evangelism)

There are other kinds of spiritual disciplines too, like meditation, sacrifice, and many more. Basically, any regular practice that draws you to abide in Christ and him in you, love others as Christ loves you, or bear much fruit is a disciple-making discipline worth your consideration.

However, because I've been helping men "grow" for a long time, I have a suggestion. One of the questions on my weekly Bible study preparation worksheet is, "What one idea, if fully understood and truly believed, could change everything?"

When it comes to spiritual growth, I would condense all the years I've spent teaching into this one idea:

A Bible, a small group, and serving someone else will solve 90 percent of your problems.

We'll go deeper, but after decades of working with men, if I am sure of anything, it's that if a man can get these three disciplines right—plus pray with and for his wife if married (but that's the next chapter!)—everything else will fall into place.

Where are you today on your spiritual journey? Maybe you can relate to one of the three kinds of men mentioned at the beginning of this chapter. Maybe you can relate to Mr. Moody.

Wherever you are on your journey, if you've made it this far it's because you are either (1) already growing, (2) want to grow, or (3) *want* to want to grow.

Now let's explore how a Bible, a small group, and serving someone else can help you become more kingdom-minded, solve your problems, and help you become the hero of your story.

The Bible

During a phone call, David said, "I'm just not sure what I believe anymore." I took that as my cue and invited him to lunch. Over lunch, I listened while David peppered me with, literally, dozens of questions. Once he started talking, it sounded like the rat-a-tat-tat of a machine gun, one question after the other, no gaps, no waiting for answers. He needed to vent.

All of David's questions are the same questions that have troubled you, me, and every other person who has ever been even remotely familiar with the Bible. You know them well:

- How can a snake talk?
- How could you get all those animals in one boat?
- What kind of God would tell a man to kill his own son (Abraham and Isaac)?
- How can a man be swallowed by a fish and then live for three days?
- How could a virgin have a baby?
- How could a man walk on water?
- And dozens more just like these.

When David's verbal flash flood finally subsided, he had bared his soul with staggering courage and vulnerability. I felt his pain. It was a sacred moment. I could tell he genuinely did hope I had an answer for these mysteries that have for centuries remained unresolved. I don't.

Instead, I had to say, "I don't have the answers to any of those questions. I'm as baffled by them as you are. Those are all the same questions I would like to have answered too."

But I was also able to tell him, "I've read the Bible cover to cover for thirty years in a row. One year, I decided to put the initials 'MA' for 'mystery abounds' at the bottom of every page where I found something I didn't understand. David, on what percentage of the pages do you think I wrote 'MA' that year?"

An engineer, he thought for a moment and then said, "I don't know. What? Maybe 30 percent?"

I laughed and said, "Try all of them! 100 percent. On one page I had scribbled MA seven times!" His first response was shock and surprise, but then relief—especially since he knew I have a seminary degree.

Then I continued. "Here's what I would like you to see. I don't understand 5 percent of the Bible, but 95 percent of it I understand just fine. I'm not going to let the few things that baffle me spoil or overshadow the 95 percent of the Bible that tells me a crystal-clear, concise, coherent, easily understood, and believable story.

"The Bible tells me we have a loving Father who relentlessly pursues his wayward children until we reconcile with him and, once we return, watches over us through thick and thin."

Why Is There Such Little Power Here?

The Bible is daunting. At roughly 780,000 words, that's about 2,500 normal book pages—equivalent to about twelve nonfiction books!

Bible reading falls into that special category of things we all know are important but struggle to execute, like diet and exercise.

With only about 10 percent of people reading the Bible with any regularity, there's little doubt that biblical illiteracy helps explain why, in our moment in history, Christianity is more *prevalent* than *powerful*.

One day, several religious leaders asked Jesus a question. They spoke about a man who was married and then died. His widow married the man's brother, and then he died too. Next she married a third brother, who also died. And so on, until she had married seven brothers. Then the leaders asked, "Whose wife will she be in heaven?"

Jesus replied, "Your problem is that you don't know the Scriptures, and you don't know the power of God" (Matthew 22:29, my paraphrase).

As you can see from the answer Jesus gave, knowing Scripture is how we release the power of God. For that to work, you need to interpret the Bible the way God intends.

Interpreting the Bible

We have a Supreme Court in the United States that meets to interpret our republic's Constitution. Generally, we see two schools of thought about how to interpret the Constitution. One school wants to interpret based on the intentions of the original authors. The other school believes the meaning of the Constitution should evolve based on experience.

The Bible is like the Christian's Constitution. To grow God's way, we need to be scrupulous to interpret the Bible based on what the original authors wrote, intended, and meant, not the good intentions of personal experience and opinion—which we know change as culture shifts occur (more on culture in chapter 9).

We should use the Bible to interpret our experience, not our experience to interpret the Bible. It's the difference between being a biblical Christian or a cultural Christian.

We're not going to discuss the principles of interpretation or study the content of the *didache* per se—that's beyond the scope of this chapter. But I do want to show you how to access your Bible for the maximum return on time invested.

First Step: Start (or Reboot) a Quiet Time

Derrick said, "I'm drifting."

"Are you doing daily devotions?" I asked.

He replied, "No, I've just been so busy lately."

Nothing else will make you feel as close to God as a time of consistent private devotions, and when inconsistent or absent, nothing will make you feel farther away.

If you don't already have a consistent quiet time (variously called personal devotions, private time, TAWG—time alone with God, etc.), start by setting aside five minutes daily to read a chapter in the Bible and say a prayer. Begin in the New Testament. Highlight passages that capture your attention. Memorize passages that speak to you for strength, courage, and faith.

Next, use the acronym "ACTS" to help you pray. "A" is for adoration. Worship God for his attributes—his love, holiness, power, majesty, beauty, kindness, mercy, grace, and goodness. "C" is for confession. Confess and ask God to forgive all known and hidden sin, and keep "short accounts" with God. "T" is for thanksgiving. Express gratitude to God for his blessings and mercies, especially things we ordinarily take for granted, like a good night's rest, daily provision, health, family, and so on. "S" is for supplication. Nothing is too big or insignificant to bring to God in prayer.

Take the Challenge: Read through the Bible in One Year

One year, I challenged the men who attend our Friday morning Bible study by saying, "Let's read through the Bible together next year! It will take about fifteen or twenty minutes per day."

More than seventy men accepted the challenge! We purchased some *One Year Bibles* and just did it. During the year, I occasionally asked, "How are you doing?" Not only did most of the men keep it up, but they were excited about how God was meeting, teaching, and changing them.

One morning, Michael walked into our Bible study with a

glowing face and greeted me warmly. In the five or six years I'd known Michael, this was a first!

"Has something changed in your life?" I asked him.

"What are you talking about?" he replied in surprise.

"Well, you seem different," I said. We exchanged pleasantries, and then he headed for the coffee and donuts.

Two weeks later, the same thing happened. Michael walked into the Bible study and gave me a surprisingly cheerful greeting.

"Okay," I said, "something's different about you."

"I don't know why you would say that," said Michael.

"Because it's true! And I'd like to understand more about it! Could we have breakfast after the meeting?" I asked.

"Sure," he said suspiciously.

Over breakfast Michael shared a lot about his early life. Then I peppered him with questions about his present life. Nothing conspicuous jumped out that would account for the change in his demeanor.

As we were about to leave, Michael mentioned a verse he had read in *The One Year Bible*. "You're doing the 'read through the Bible program'?" I asked.

"Yes. I've been reading the Bible every day. I'm up to date," he said. Unbeknown to the other men at his table, Michael had accepted the challenge to read through the Bible. He was right up to date!

"That's it!" I said. "That's the correlation! You've been reading through God's Word on your own for the first time, your life is changing, and you're not even aware of it. This is awesome!"

Michael was being transformed by the powerful Word of God. Michael was encouraged, and the experience reinforced his desire to know God better.

If you would like to accept the challenge, you can purchase *The One Year Bible*—it includes daily readings from the Old

Testament, the New Testament, Psalms, and Proverbs. Better yet, purchase a stock of *One Year Bibles* and get your small group to take the challenge with you.

Or you can download *The One Year Bible* reading plan from the internet and look up the texts in your existing Bible (www .oneyearbibleonline.com). The online plan is available in numerous languages and dozens of translations.

You can start with today's date. You don't need to wait until January 1.

Set a Routine

What is the best time of day, place, frequency, and amount of time for you to read the Bible? The best time of the day is when you are fresh. My "fresh" time to read is early in the morning. I make a cup of coffee and settle into my chair for an unhurried time of prayer and reading the Word of God. If it fits your personality, it's a good idea to have a set schedule.

Daily Bible reading makes sense for the same reasons we recharge our cell phones. Of course, things come up–an argument with your spouse, an alarm that doesn't go off, early meetings, or cranky kids. On average, I read about five days a week.

How much time you spend reading is completely a matter of personal preference, but I've had men tell me they set aside five minutes, fifteen minutes, thirty minutes, an hour, and some men even longer.

Pray When Reading

It's a good idea to pray when you read. How I pray connects to the guiding principle I established for my personal life: *I will commit myself to a life of devotion and study of God, then speak, teach, and write about what I'm learning.*

A life of devotion is *communion* (loving God) and a life of study is *discipleship* (knowing God). In other words, I want loving and knowing God to be my highest and best thought in every situation. So when I start my quiet times, I ask God to meet with and abide in us, as we come to meet with and abide in him— his much-loved sons and daughters, disciples, friends, servants, temples, vessels, and charges.

Oswald Chambers suggests, "Unless in the first waking moment of the day you learn to fling the door wide back and let God in, you will work on a wrong level all day; but swing the door wide open and pray to your Father in secret, and every public thing will be stamped with the presence of God."[3]

What to Do When Your Mind Wanders

What will you do when your mind wanders? My mind wanders all the time. And to be honest, I like it. There are four possibilities when my mind wanders: the world, the flesh, the devil, or the Spirit.

When your mind wanders, you have to figure out which voice is speaking. If it is the world, the flesh, or the devil, then of course you want to reel it back in.

However, if I read a Scripture and my mind goes racing to a relationship that's not right, or I am convicted of a sin or prompted to some good deed, then that is the Spirit, and I happily let my mind go there. When I read a phrase or sentence that impacts me, I like to linger awhile, letting the Word soak into my soul.

What if your mind wanders because you're tired and exhausted? When I get that way, I try to read out loud. If I still can't concentrate, I just stop and live to read another day!

What You Can Do When You Get Stuck

What can you do if you fall behind on a reading plan? If you're like most of us, you may at some point

- get bogged down in Leviticus and Numbers (They read like the tech manual for a piece of software. Fortunately, we live by a more recent version of the software. Thank God for our free upgrade to Jesus.)
- find yourself reading and rereading the same sentence over and over
- find yourself daydreaming about your favorite team
- fall asleep reading about the details of constructing the tabernacle
- wonder, *What's up with all that blood sprinkling?*

It's easy to fall behind in the daily readings.

- end of January—three days behind, feel guilty but plan to make it up
- end of February—a week behind, starting to gnaw on you, you plan to catch up in one sitting
- end of March—ten days behind, you're thinking, *This isn't working.*
- end of April—emergency at work, three weeks behind, you're about to give it up
- Then once you get a month or so behind, it's tempting to just quit altogether.

Whenever you start to fall behind, give yourself a "get out of jail free" pass. Simply start over with today's reading and forget about the days you missed. You may use this "get out of jail free" pass again anytime during the year. It's grace.

If you're still having a hard time keeping up, here are some ideas. First, just read the days you can, and forget about the other days. Or read a smaller section. For example, just read the New Testament this year (another year, if you want, you can add back the Old Testament). The New Testament has 260 chapters—that's a chapter a day, five days a week.

Why am I suggesting these cuts? God would rather spend a little time with you in his Word than no time at all.

Now let's turn to small groups.

A Small Group

Someone once asked Billy Graham, the most revered preacher in America for more than half a century, "If you were a pastor of a large church in a principal city, what would be your plan of action?"

I would have imagined that Mr. Graham would outline a mass evangelistic plan to take the city by storm. Instead, in *The Master Plan of Evangelism*, it's reported that he answered, "One of the first things I would do would be to get a small group of eight or ten or twelve people around me that would meet a few hours a week and pay the price! It would cost them something in time and effort. I would share with them everything I have, over a period of years. Then I would actually have twelve ministers among the laypeople who in turn could take eight or ten or twelve more and teach them."[4]

Not a bad idea. It certainly worked for Jesus! A small group was unmistakably his primary discipleship model. Jesus used a small group as his venue for spiritual growth. Jesus launched his divine plan to redeem mankind by making disciples in a single small group. Impressive. The question, of course, is why would he do that? Why a small group?

Why Small Groups?

Jesus knew that most meaningful change takes place in the context of small group relationships—men sharpening men with truth, encouraging each other for the daily battle, and sticking with each other over the long haul.

Small groups gained momentum in the seventeenth century, when Philip Jacob Spener (1635–1705), the father of German Pietism, initiated a series of reforms. Central to his method was the *collegia pietatis*—"small groups" for Bible study, prayer, and intimacy that he hoped would renew a staid and arid church. His plan worked.

Even secularists understand the value of small groups. Anthropologist Margaret Mead said, "Never doubt that a small group of thoughtful, committed citizens can change the world; indeed, it's the only thing that ever has."[5]

Today, although most men believe in God, every study I've seen shows less than 10 percent of men are involved in any kind of ongoing discipleship.

That is tragic, because mission number one for Christian service is to make disciples. But often, we're so busy treating symptoms screaming for immediate attention—partner problems, wayward children, gossip, ethical failures, apathy, backbiting, etc.—that we fail to treat the underlying disease. It's like trying to cure cancer with morphine. Sure, morphine takes away the pain for a while, but it does nothing to cure the patient.

God wants to cure us, not merely anesthetize our pain. The cure is Jesus Christ, and small groups are vital to his plan. Jesus started a small group to bring his first disciples to full maturity. *No other method has ever been shown to be even remotely as effective at changing men's lives.*

What can a small group do for you that you can get no other way?

What You Can Get in a Small Group That You Can't Get Any Other Way

After my wife and the Bible, God has used small groups more than anything else to change my life. Here's my small group resume:

- two weekly couples home groups, each lasting a few years
- four weekly one-on-one meetings with different men (totaling more than seventy years of weekly meetings!)
- a monthly leader's group from our Friday morning Bible study (we stopped meeting for about six years and lost something, so we started back up)

So much—perhaps most—of the caring, sharing, learning, growth, encouragement, accountability, prayer, and friendship I've experienced has taken place in these small groups.

What makes small groups special is that the size is manageable. You feel like you can really get to know the others. And, just as importantly, you feel like they can get to know you well enough that they *really* understand you and *genuinely* care about what happens in your life.

What kind of small group is right for you? You want to be part of a group that feels like you're coming home to a family who really cares about you, not going to a job where you're going to get fired if you can't perform. Christianity should feel like a home, not a job.

What should a small group do? There are so many kinds of small group structures—Bible studies, video Bible studies, book studies, prayer groups, fellowships, recovery groups, service projects, mission teams, accountability groups, and many combinations thereof. Some groups have a set time like eight weeks or one year. Others do not have a set ending time. Some groups plan to disciple men and multiply, others don't. There's no one "right" way to meet as a small group.

That said, some groups do better because they are "doing life together." They share what's *really* going on; they keep the group small enough so there's time to really get to know each other; they study the Bible together; they pray for each other, hold each other accountable, and check on each other when it's the right thing to do. We call it "life-on-life discipleship."

Sound attractive? I hope so! That's all we'll say for now, but what if you're not in a small group? Would you like to start one? In the chapter on friendships, I'll give you a step-by-step guide on "How to Start a Weekly Men's Small Group."

In addition to a Bible and a small group, the third thing that will help you solve 90 percent of your problems is serving someone else. You'll be amused by how I learned this lesson.

Serving Someone Else

Early in my spiritual journey, I was depressed about something and kept moping around the house. Finally one day my wife said, "Do you know what your problem is?"

Oh, that's just great, I thought. *What's my problem?*

Before I could tell her I didn't care what my problem was, nor did I want to talk about it, she said, "Your problem is self-pity. You're too focused on your own problems. You just need to get out of the house and go help someone else with a bigger problem."

Boom!

So that's what I did. I went to an urban ministry here in my hometown and offered to help. By the time I left after that very first visit, the cloud had lifted.

God wants every Christian man to have a personal ministry. "For we are God's handiwork, created in Christ Jesus to do good works, which God prepared in advance for us to do" (Ephesians 2:10).

Serving someone else is one of the chief identifying marks of a disciple. "This is to my Father's glory, that you bear much fruit, showing yourselves to be my disciples" (John 15:8).

Becoming aware of your own spiritual gifts will (1) help you understand how and where you fit into the body of Christ, (2) help you set priorities for service, and (3) give you direction for developing a personal ministry. Basically, you want to answer the question, "What makes my heart beat fast and puts a smile on my face?"

SPIRITUAL GIFTS ASSESSMENT TOOL

It would be foolish to become a salesman if you'd rather fix computers. In the same way we pursue vocational employment based on motivated interests, aptitudes, and abilities, we pursue spiritual service based on the way God has wired us with the gifts of the Holy Spirit.

These gifts are not only for church work. They can be used in *any* ministry, including church, home, and work.

While theologians and teachers sometimes differ on how to precisely classify and name these gifts, they are often divided into *service* gifts, *speaking* gifts, and *signifying* gifts. Here are the spiritual gifts mentioned in Scripture.

Service Gifts

Service gifts are the ligaments and muscle tissue that hold the church of Jesus Christ together. Service gifts are often low-profile, behind-the-scene gifts. They include showing mercy, service (or helps), hospitality, giving, administration, leadership, faith, and discernment.

People who serve are eager for God to receive the credit for whatever good comes. "If anyone *serves*, they should do so with the strength God provides, so that in all things God may be praised through Jesus Christ" (1 Peter 4:11, emphasis added). The following examples (along with speaking and signifying lists) are adapted from the work of Carl Smith, Kenneth O. Gangel, and Leslie B. Flynn.[6]

_____ **Mercy:** Special ability to show sympathy to the suffering saints. Meals to the sick, hospital visits, phone calls, emails, texts, and visits to the hurting. A vocation as a nurse or physician.

_____ **Service:** Special ability to joyfully serve behind the scenes. Set up chairs, serve as an usher, assist leaders. A vocation in customer service or landscape maintenance.

_____ **Hospitality:** Special desire to offer home, food, and lodging. Host missionaries, Bible studies, singles for dinner. A vocation in food service or tourism.

_____ **Giving:** Special desire and financial ability to give above and beyond a tithe. Generosity toward youth mission trips, deacon fund offerings, parachurch ministries, a suit for the pastor. A vocation in philanthropy.

_____ **Administration:** Special ability to orchestrate program details. Committee work, volunteer for church office, conference/seminar supervision. A vocation in business.

_____ **Leadership:** Special ability to preside or govern wisely. Boards of Christian ministries, visible roles, elders, deacons, committee chairmen, run nursery program, fundraising. A vocation in management.

_____ **Faith:** Vision for new projects that need doing and perseverance to see them through. Building programs, new ministries. A vocation as an entrepreneur.

_____ **Discernment:** Ability to detect error. Meet with teachers who may be teaching incorrectly, write letters to the editor. A vocation in law.

Speaking Gifts

People who have been given speaking gifts are able to help equip others to have a personal ministry of service. "So Christ himself gave the apostles, the prophets, the evangelists, the pastors and teachers, *to equip his people for works of service*, so that the body of Christ may be built up" (Ephesians 4:11–12, emphasis added).

Speaking gifts include knowledge, wisdom, preaching, teaching, evangelism, apostleship, shepherding, and encouragement. "If anyone *speaks*, they should do so as one who speaks the very words of God" (1 Peter 4:11, emphasis added). Here are definitions and examples of the spiritual gifts of speaking:

_____ *Knowledge:* Spiritual ability to search and acquire scriptural truth. Academic pursuits, writing, teaching. A vocation as an educator.

_____ *Wisdom:* Special insight into applications of knowledge. Counseling, teaching, discussion group leader, accountability groups, friendship. A vocation as a counselor or personal coach.

_____ *Preaching:* Special ability to rightly proclaim and expound God's truth. Preachers, lay preachers. A vocation as a public speaker.

_____ *Teaching:* Special ability to explain Scripture in an edifying way. Sunday school teachers, Bible studies, home groups, children, youth programs. A vocation as a teacher.

_____ *Evangelism:* Special ability to clearly present the gospel to nonbelievers. Sunday night church visitation program, share faith with contacts on job, sponsor outreach events. A vocation as a salesman.

_____ **_Apostleship:_** Special ability to begin new works. Missionaries, church planters, Christian service organizations. A vocation as an entrepreneur.

_____ **_Shepherding:_** Unique ability to care for a flock of believers over the long haul. Pastors, elders, nursery program. A vocation as a manager.

_____ **_Encouragement:_** Special skill to inspire, encourage, and comfort. This may be through friendship, counseling, writing letters, and the like. All vocations.

Signifying Gifts

The signifying gifts are miracles, healing, speaking in tongues, and the interpretation of tongues.

_____ **_Miracles:_** Spiritual ability to actuate the supernatural intervention of God against the laws of nature.

_____ **_Healing:_** Spiritual agency of God in curing illness and disease and restoring to health supernaturally.

_____ **_Tongues:_** Spiritual ability to speak in a language foreign to speaker.

_____ **_Interpretation of Tongues:_** Spiritual ability to interpret the message of one speaking in tongues.

If you've never studied or don't understand your own spiritual gifts, follow these suggested steps:

1. Study and reflect. Study the four passages of Scripture that deal with spiritual gifts: Romans 12:3–8; 1 Corinthians 12:1–31; Ephesians 4:11–13; 1 Peter 4:9–11. You may want to study the context by examining the verses before and after these specific references.

Your gifts will usually be related to the following, so reflect on and answer these questions:

What are your natural abilities?

_____

_____

What are your motivated interests?

_____

_____

What is your previous successful ministry involvement
(if applicable)

_____

Where have you received positive feedback from other Christians?

_____

What is the burden, or calling, you sense?

_____

_____

2. Narrow your list. Now that you have studied the Scripture passages and answered these questions, it's time to narrow the list to the specific spiritual gifts that you "think" you possess or "possibly" may possess. How do you do that?

I've included a blank space in front of each spiritual gift above. You can write in the book, but for the reason mentioned in the "Feedback" section below, I suggest you write on a photocopy of the list. Now mark each gift in the blank space provided, using the following legend:

Y = Yes. I think I possess this spiritual gift.
M = Maybe. I may possess this spiritual gift.
N = No. I do not possess this spiritual gift.
D = Don't know. I don't know if I possess this spiritual gift.

3. Rank your answers. Now that you've sifted through the list of gifts, you should have one or more "Y" and "M" notations in the blanks. Write each of those spiritual gifts in the following spaces:

_____

_____

_____

_____

Now rank these in order of priority based on what you know at this time. Put a "1" next to the gift with which you most identify, a "2" by your second choice, and so on. This is provisional—you are still exploring.

4. Seek feedback. An excellent way to assist in determining your spiritual gifts is to ask your Christian friends for help. Ask a few friends to rank you, using the same legend you used in the above section, "Narrow your list." Make enough additional copies of the spiritual gifts above for each friend. Compare the results to your own assessment. Should you add any spiritual gifts to your exploratory list?

Explore. Now it's time to explore the possibilities! Take special training in your potential areas of giftedness. Experiment with different ministries. Which ones energize you? Which ones are drudgery? In what areas are you being affirmed by other people? Discovering your spiritual gifts will inevitably open up a whole new realm of joy in the Lord.

To know God is to serve him, and the happiest people in the world are those who know their spiritual gifts and are using them for the glory of God.

If you want to grow, focus on a Bible, a small group, and serving someone else. That will solve 90 percent of your problems. Is that hyperbole? Yes. Is it a generalization? Yes. Is it true? Yes.

A CALL TO ACTION

In this chapter, you've received three separate calls to action—to read the Bible for yourself, to be part of a small group, and to serve someone. The Reflection and Small Group Discussion Questions at the end will help you think through how you may want to respond. Here's a prayer to finish off this chapter. And be sure to answer the questions.

Our dearest Father, we come to you and humble ourselves. We want to grow in maturity and knowledge and wisdom and power. We want to be transformed. We want to renew our minds. We want to know your good, pleasing, and perfect will for our lives. Lord, I have just read that a Bible, a small group, and serving someone else will solve 90 percent of my problems. I pray that you would help me to fully understand and truly believe it. Change me for your glory. Show me the next steps you want me to take. Help me grow into a more kingdom-minded man. I make this prayer, Jesus, in your wonderful and precious name. Amen.

Turning now to our next topic, if men say their number one issue is spiritual growth, what do you think men who minister to men would say is the number one issue? That's the subject of our next chapter!

Reflection and Small Group Discussion Questions

1. The big idea for this chapter is, "A Bible, a small group, and serving someone else will solve 90 percent of your problems." It's hyperbole, of course, but can you give an example of how one or more of these three aspects of personal spiritual growth has changed your life?

2. What do the following verses say about:
   - the Bible? Hebrews 4:12
   - small groups? Hebrews 10:25
   - serving someone else? Hebrew 13:20–21

3. Rate yourself from 1 to 10 on the following:
   - _4_ Reading the Bible
   - _0_ Small group participation
   - _7_ Serving others

What is the one area that you think would most accelerate your spiritual maturity, knowledge, wisdom, and power? Do you plan to do anything differently and, if so, what is it?

Heb. 4:12 It has the wisdom to help me run thru everyday life - the words are good for today & tomorrow & the rest of my life
Heb 10:25 - getting to know the people - worship together - support during the different times
Heb 20-21 - help me to be "molded" like God to help others - doing His will
Serving others - continue to help any way I can - If I can

FOUR

MARRIAGE

Finding a New Best Friend in My Wife

He who finds a wife finds what is good
and receives favor from the LORD.

PROVERBS 18:22

> Most marriage problems would disappear if we would simply speak to our wives with the same kindness, courtesy, forethought, and respect with which we speak to our coworkers.

When my wife and I fell in love, I was racing motorcycles. My dream was to own a motorcycle dealership and travel around the country winning motocross races on the weekends.

One day not long after we started dating, she phoned her parents in Miami and said, "Mom and Dad, I think I've met the man I'm going to marry."

Her father said, "That's great, honey. What does he want to do?"

She said, "Dad, it's so exciting! We're going to travel around the country and he's going to be racing motorcycles and someday we're going to own a motorcycle dealership!"

Just what every father wants to hear.

A few months later, I bought Patsy a 100cc dirt bike so we could go trail riding together. Watching her ride, I knew in my heart that she was only doing it for me.

Soon we married and went on our honeymoon. A couple of weeks after we got back, I said, "Hey, let's go dirt biking this weekend!"

She said, "I tell you what . . . I've got some things I need to get settled here in our apartment. Why don't you go by yourself this weekend?"

Would you believe it? Once we were married, she never ever once got on a motorcycle again!

When we were dating, every day I would pull over to the side of the road somewhere and pick a flower for Patsy as a token of my love.

Would you believe it? Once we were married, I never ever once picked her a roadside flower again!

WHAT NEEDS TO HAPPEN NOW THAT THE HONEYMOON IS OVER?

Once the honeymoon is over, once the dirt bikes and daily flowers come to a natural conclusion, adjustments need to be made. It's a new season to settle down, set up a home, build a life together, understand each other's needs, synchronize your lives, and find a rhythm for living together.

The two of you are setting up some ground rules, figuring out each other's hot buttons and how not to push them. You're answering questions such as, What's going to be the division of labor in our home? How are we going to support each other? What is my mate's love language? How can we best encourage, comfort, and console each other and take the time to do that?

You're working out a sex life, having children, going to work, and figuring out how you're going to deal with money. You're learning how to resolve conflicts, discovering that you can't control each other and be happy, and working out the important skill of asking and giving forgiveness. Plus, learning how to leave time for having some fun together. It's a lot to handle.

By the end of your first year of marriage, your romantic notion of what it would be like to share a bedroom has been jolted back to reality. As I once heard author Florence Littauer say, "We are attracted to marry each other's strengths, but then go home to live with each other's weaknesses."

THE #1 PROBLEM AND THE #1 OPPORTUNITY FOR MOST MEN

No man plans to fail in marriage. No man ever went into a marriage thinking, *I wonder how quickly I can blow this up?* Every man who ever exchanged vows pictured himself heroically providing for and protecting a woman for whom he would willingly give his life.

Yet in spite of our intentions, if we put men's marriage problems in one stack and *all* the other problems men face in a second stack, the marriage stack alone is still higher than all of men's other problems combined.

Easily the number one problem for most men is that their marriages are not working the way God intended.

As one of the twenty-four men from our storyboard group pointed out, "It feels like we need to hear why our marriages really trump the other priorities in our lives."

But there's more. The issues most couples struggle with during their first year of marriage are, by degrees, the same issues they'll still be struggling with five, ten, or twenty years down the road.

How about you? If you could peer into a crystal ball and see ten or twenty years down the road, what do you think your marriage will look like if you continue your current course?

I have some great news for you. The number one opportunity for most married men is how a surprisingly few, but strategic, course corrections can dramatically alter where your marriage will end up in ten or twenty years.

Maybe you're newly married, maybe you've been married for many years, maybe you're divorced, maybe you are thinking about getting married or getting a divorce, or maybe you're separated. Whatever your personal situation, I pray God will use this chapter to give you a fresh, optimistic outlook for your wife and marriage.

WHY MEN GET MARRIED

Many have sought to explain why men get married, but I've never seen a more succinct explanation than this:

The LORD God said, "It is not good for the man to be alone.
I will make a helper suitable for him."

Genesis 2:18

That is why a man leaves his father and mother and is united
to his wife, and they become one flesh.

Genesis 2:24

Men don't like to be alone. It's in our nature. And we need
help. It's in our nature. So God created women and instituted the
miracle of marriage.

Marriage is the beautiful, mysterious fusion of a man and
a woman into what the Bible intriguingly calls "one flesh." For
those God calls to marry or remarry, marriage is the Eiffel Tower
of human relationships, majestically towering high above every
other relationship.

By doing marriage God's way, you can be your wife's best
friend, and she yours. The starting point is to understand how
she processes differently than you do, and why.

THE WAY GOD MADE HER

One day I told my wife I was going to teach our son what makes
a wife tick. She said, "Good luck!"

Genesis 3:16 says, "To the woman he said, 'I will make your
pains in childbearing very severe; with painful labor you will give
birth to children. Your *desire* will be for your husband, and he will
rule over you'" (emphasis added).

As part of her "nature," your wife is going to give you the first
place in her life. A wife's greatest need is for intimacy with her
husband. That's her natural instinct. When her "desire" for you
is led by the Holy Spirit, nothing is more beautiful and precious.

However, the full sense of Hebrew word for *desire* is best understood as "a desire bordering on disease." Because of the Fall, her desire for you can be corrupted or taken advantage of. For example, she might be susceptible to manipulation, jealousy, being too clingy, too needy, worry, or wanting to control. No doubt that's why the Bible instructs husbands,

> Husbands, love your wives and do not be harsh with them.
>
> *Colossians 3:19*

> Husbands, in the same way be considerate as you live with your wives, and treat them with respect as the weaker partner and as heirs with you of the gracious gift of life, so that nothing will hinder your prayers.
>
> *1 Peter 3:7*

Cut her some slack. The Fall has affected her just as profoundly, though differently from you. For you:

> "Cursed is the ground because of you;
>> through painful toil you will eat food from it
>> all the days of your life.
> It will produce thorns and thistles for you,
>> and you will eat the plants of the field.
> By the sweat of your brow
>> you will eat your food
> until you return to the ground."
>
> *Genesis 3:17–19*

Just as you need her support when you feel the prick of thorns, she needs you to be tender with her. Now that you know what she needs, how do you give it to her?

SACRIFICIAL LOVE IS YOUR PRIMARY ROLE

My wife's parents moved to Orlando, and my father-in-law, Ed, and I became weekly lunch buddies and best friends for the last seven years of his life.

Not long after they moved here, my mother-in-law, June, needed to permanently move into the nursing care wing of their retirement community. Ed turned his apartment into a camp-site. He slept there but spent as much of every day as he could in his wife's room. For her part, June said, "I just want to be with Ed."

She was his top priority, and because of that, they were best friends. As the shadows of twilight fell across them, the only thing they really wanted was to be together. May I say that again? *As the shadows of twilight fell across them, the only thing they really wanted was to be together.*

Ed's love illustrates the primary, longest, almost only, and definitely most elegant instruction the Bible offers a man about his role as a husband:

Husbands, love your wives, *just as* Christ loved the church and gave himself up for her to make her holy, cleansing her by the washing with water through the word, and to present her to himself as a radiant church, without stain or wrinkle or any other blemish, but holy and blameless. In this same way, husbands ought to love their wives as their own bodies. He who loves his wife loves himself. After all, no one ever hated their own body, but they feed and care for their body, just as Christ does the church—for we are members of his body. "For this reason a man will leave his father and mother and be united to his wife, and the two will become one flesh." This is a profound mystery—but I am talking about Christ and the church.

Ephesians 5:25–32, emphasis added

The way Jesus loves his bride is the template for how we love our brides. Notice the exhortation to sacrificially love your bride *just as* ("equal to" or "in the same way") Jesus loved and gave himself to his bride, the church (the body of Christ).

She means everything to Jesus. He held nothing back from her. He sacrificed everything he had to serve her. He was willing to die for her. In short, his bride was his top priority, and that's what Scripture wants us to imitate:

After God, but before all others, make your bride your top priority.

I've written three books on marriage and chapters on marriage in several other books that contain hundreds of marriage ideas. Frankly, I think—and this is the big idea for this chapter—most marriage problems would disappear if we would simply speak to our wives with the same kindness, courtesy, forethought, and respect with which we speak to our coworkers.

That said, here are some practical ideas to help you do just that—adopting the 70 percent mind-set, praying *for* and *with* your wife, making deposits into her emotional bank account, and making your wife your best friend. Do these and you'll be well on your way to making your wife your top priority. And by God's grace, a wife who one day many years from now might say, "I just want to be with you."

The 70 Percent Mind-Set

Most people would agree that Billy Graham was one of the most exemplary Christian men who ever walked the face of the planet. But his wife, Ruth, once quipped, "I've never considered divorce. Murder, yes, but not divorce."[1] Not even Billy Graham had a "perfect" marriage.

You're going to have Billy Graham days.

Where does marital disappointment come from? Somewhere in the relationship you have an expectation of your wife that isn't being met—appearance, level of effort, sex, and so forth.

And to keep it real, some days you feel like you're going to explode. "I can't believe that I was so stupid to marry this woman!" or "What was I thinking?" Those are extreme, of course, but we all have those kinds of days. Of course, your wife does too.

How do we keep a few disappointments from ruining an otherwise good thing?

As a general rule, *all disappointment is the result of unmet expectations.* For example, suppose you received a bonus of $1,000. If you thought you were going to get $500, you would be ecstatic. But you'd be terribly disappointed if you had been expecting $2,000. The bonus is $1,000 regardless. The only difference is what you expected.

So my first suggestion to help you make your wife your top priority is to adjust your expectations. If you set realistic expectations, you won't feel like you're getting "less" from each other than you expected. So, what's realistic?

Family systems scholar Edwin Friedman said, "In reality, no human marriage gets a rating of more than 70%."[2] What he meant was that humming along at about 70 percent of potential is the norm.

Let's do a thought experiment. If you calculate 70 percent of seven days, that's 4.9. Let's call it five out of seven days. In a "normal" marriage and family system, you will experience marital satisfaction for five out of seven days. But a couple of days a week are likely to be a little off—mood swings, job woes, money pressure, the stress of children. In other words, even the most successful marriage will only be symptom-free about 70 percent of the time.

Both my wife and I think we have a great marriage. When I

first ran across this 70 percent rule, I asked her to read the page in the book. She did and, without looking up, said definitively, "That sounds about right."

We've adopted "the 70 percent mind-set," and we both have found that lowering our expectations of each other has increased our marital satisfaction. Now I only want to murder her one day a week instead of two (kidding!).

You may be wondering, *Is that as good as it gets?* But a better thought would be, *Wow, maybe my marriage is better than I thought!* If you will dwell on this 70 percent number, I think in time you will be encouraged by it.

Why just 70 percent? It's the Fall. We see each other through the veil of our sinful natures. It takes grace to make a marriage work. No person is ideal. Our wives can be controlling, neglectful, strong-willed, pouty, unexpressive, unappreciative, and on and on. So can we.

The main way I have personally put "the 70 percent mind-set" into practice is by repeating a sentence for which I have paid a big price. But before I tell you the sentence, let me tell you how it came about.

One day my wife said out of the blue, "I don't feel safe with you anymore." I was devastated, but I knew why. For a few years I had been putting a lot of pressure on her to exercise more—one of my personal values. My repeated "encouragements" were instead taken as jabs that made her feel like she wasn't good enough for me the way she was. That pressure made her feel like she had to perform—that my love for her was conditional.

When she said that, I figured I could apologize, change course, and that would take care of it. And so that's what I did. But to my complete surprise, she didn't respond. In fact, it took three very long years until one day she said, "I feel safe with you again." During those years, the Lord repeatedly revealed my sinful nature to me. I repented for pressuring her and also for assuming I could fix it overnight. And now, here is the sentence I came up with during those three long years:

"I let you be you, and you let me be me."

Today, after many years of repetition, it's just part of who we are—both of us. It's a habit. It's part of my worldview. A guiding principle. Consider giving it a try. It's an easy-to-remember way to manage your expectations.

Adopting the 70 percent mind-set is the first suggestion for making your wife your top priority after God. The second suggestion is to pray *for* and *with* her.

Pray *for* Your Wife

David Delk and I wrote a book, *The Marriage Prayer*, in which we outlined a sixty-eight-word prayer that captures the essence of the Bible's teaching about marriage. There is a version for husbands to pray for their wives and a version for wives to pray for their husbands. Here's the husband's version:

> *Father,*
>> *I said, "'Til death do us part"—I want to mean it.*
>> *Help me love You more than her,*
>> *and her more than anyone or anything else.*
>> *Help me bring her into Your presence today.*
>> *Make us one, like You are three in one.*
>> *I want to hear her, cherish her, and serve her—*
>> *so she would love you more and we can bring You glory.*
>> *Amen.*

In my human pride, I didn't think I "personally" needed to pray this prayer, but felt I had a duty to pray for my wife because I was, after all, recommending it to men!

Within weeks, strange things started to happen. I began asking,

"Can I get you another cup of coffee?" "Would you like me to take out the trash?" and dozens of similar questions that were new for me.

One day, I saw empty Splenda packets stuck to the bottom of the wastebasket and made it my business to retrieve them. The next thing I remember was standing there wondering, *What just happened?* And then it dawned on me. A phrase from the marriage prayer went through my mind: "I want to hear her, cherish her, and serve her—so she would love you more."

The Evolution of the Marriage Prayer

After a few months of praying "I want to mean it" and "Help me love you more than her, and her more than anyone or anything else," another change came over me.

I realized I didn't merely "want" to mean it. I *did* mean it! And I didn't need God to "help" me to love him and her. I *did* love them both most of all!

So I changed the first two sentences and started praying:

> *"Father,*
> *I said, "'Til death do us part"—I ~~want to~~ mean it.*
> *~~Help me~~ I love You more than her,*
> *and her more than anyone or anything else.*

At that point, I was sure God had shown me all there was to see. But there was more!

Praying in the Key of We

Two years ago, I had an epiphany while reading the Lord's Prayer. I was struck by how "other-ish" the prayer sounded. Jesus taught us to pray "us" and "we" prayers, not "I" and "me" prayers. See for yourself how *nine* times Jesus tells us to pray on behalf of others as well as ourselves:

"This, then, is how you should pray:

> "'*Our* Father in heaven,
> hallowed be your name,
> your kingdom come,
> your will be done,
>> on earth as it is in heaven.
> Give *us* today *our* daily bread.
> And forgive *us our* debts,
>> as *we* also have forgiven *our* debtors.
> And lead *us* not into temptation,
>> but deliver *us* from the evil one.'"
>
> *Matthew 6:9–13, emphasis added*

Imagine if Jesus had taught us only to pray, "Give *me* my daily bread. And forgive *me* my debts. And lead *me* not into temptation, but deliver *me* from the evil one."

At that point, I realized most of my prayers were prayed in the key of me. So I started praying all my prayers in the key of *we*.

Instantly, the aperture controlling the field of vision for my mind's eye was radically opened. Instead of praying just for myself and a few others, suddenly the images of literally hundreds of people started passing through my mind as I prayed. It was like I had been diseased with spiritual tunnel vision but was suddenly healed. It was like taking off a telephoto lens and putting on a wide-angle lens.

So I adjusted and started praying the marriage prayer, this time in the key of *we*.

The result is a prayer you can pray too. Depending on whether you're at the "we *want* to mean it" or the "we *mean* it" stage, here are two versions of the marriage prayer. Why not give it a try?

The Marriage Prayer: We Version

Father,
    we said, "'Til death do us part"—we want to mean it.
    Help us love You more than each other,
    and each other more than anyone or anything else.
    Help us bring each other into Your presence today.
    Make us one, like You are three in one.
    We want to hear each other, cherish each other, and
serve each other—
    so we both would love you more and bring You glory.
    Amen.

The Marriage Prayer: Pro Version

Father,
    we said, "'Til death do us part"—we ~~want to~~ mean it.
    ~~Help us~~ We love You more than each other,
    and each other more than anyone or anything else.
    Help us bring each other into Your presence today.
    Make us one, like You are three in one.
    We want to hear each other, cherish each other, and
serve each other—
    so we both would love you more and bring You glory.
    Amen.

Pray *with* Your Wife

In addition to praying for your wife, you can also pray *with* her. You may find it surprising, but also a relief, that not many men actually pray with their wives. For example, I recently did a video chat with one of our video Bible study groups that has been meeting for seventeen years. Of the twelve men on the call, only two of them said they pray with their wives.

Praying with your wife sounds more intimidating than it is in practice. You don't need to pray together for a long time. For example, Patsy and I pray for about one to three minutes in the morning. And if we miss a morning, we don't worry about it. I'm usually the one who prays. She'll pray if I ask, but that's not her thing and she really would rather have me pray. Still, every now and then I will say, "Why don't you pray today," and she does.

You don't need a special place or time. For example, we just pray on the spot when we're ready to start our day.

You can pray about anything you want, and you don't need to do much, if any, preparation. We always pray for our children and grandchildren. We pray looking back with thanks and gratitude, and then pray forward in supplication for people, situations, and daily tasks.

Also, we pray over the dinner meal, though we usually eat breakfast and lunch on our own.

As you can see, it doesn't take a lot of effort, but it can make a profound difference.

Praying the Marriage Prayer with Your Wife

I've saved the best for last! I pray the marriage prayer for my wife virtually every day, but once or twice a month, I pray it with her. Adjust to your own taste, but I've found about once every two weeks is a nice interval. That's often enough to really have an impact but not so often that it becomes rote.

You can pray either the *we* version or the *pro* version.

Caution: You may find it nerve-racking to pray the marriage prayer out loud with your wife at first. That's understandable. Because this prayer can do so much good, the spiritual opposition is so fierce. Go ahead and push through the fear. I can't think of *anything* that has warmed my heart toward my wife and made me feel more connected to her than praying the marriage prayer with her out loud. Give it a try!

Along with adopting the 70 percent mind-set and praying for and with your wife, here is a peerless idea.

The Emotional Bank Account

The third suggestion and most practical idea I've ever heard of and written about is the *emotional bank account*. The concept is quite simple. Every human being—you, your wife, or the woman you're going to marry—has an emotional bank.

Picture a vault in her chest. With every interaction you have with her, you are either making a deposit into her emotional bank account or making a withdrawal. Every word you speak, every gesture you make, every minute that you give her or don't. *Everything* about your relationship is either a deposit or a withdrawal.

Let's look at a couple of examples. You come home from work. It has been a long day. You're exhausted. You don't want to engage with anyone. You have felt this way before, and you have developed a system—a way of letting your wife know that you don't have anything left to give. And so, as you walk through the door, you let out a deep, heavy growl that resembles the sound of a large zoo animal, signaling to her, "I've had a tough day. I really don't want to be bothered by anybody and anything. Whatever you had to go through today, I've had to go through a lot worse so don't bother me."

So, is this a deposit or a withdrawal from your wife's emotional bank account? Okay. You get the picture.

Now let's suppose it's the next morning, and because you feel so guilt-ridden for being so grumpy, you decide to bring her breakfast in bed with an apology. Is that a withdrawal or a deposit? Obviously, that's a deposit.

As I said, everything is a deposit or withdrawal, but a few deposits are better than others. Focus your deposits where your wife most appreciates them. To accomplish that, you'll need to know her love language.

Gary Chapman wrote that there are five love languages:

- words of affirmation
- quality time
- receiving gifts
- acts of service
- physical touch[3]

Of these, we each have one or two main ways we prefer to be loved.

However, a cautionary tale is in order! That's because our tendency is to love the way we want to be loved, not the way our mate wants to be loved.

For example, my wife loves running errands for me, like going to the store or picking up dry cleaning. That gives her great pleasure, because that's her love language. And I appreciate it so much, but my love language is quality time. In other words, I feel most loved when we're together, not because she ran to the store—as nice as that is.

On the other hand, since I know her love language is service, I try to do chores that come up around the house without procrastinating, such as changing bulbs, unloading the groceries, fixing things, etc. Since I'm not handy, those chores are not high on my list. I have to substitute discipline for a lack of natural interest. But when I see how much loving her in her love language means to her, it's more than worth the effort.

Couple the emotional bank account with Chapman's five love languages, and you have a focused way to make deposits.

The last and possibly most important idea is to intentionally set out to be a best friend to your wife.

Be Your Wife's Best Friend

Once I conducted a survey among the wives of the men in our Bible study to find out what *they* thought were the most important issues facing their marriages.

The primary response was, "We don't spend enough time together." Many also responded, "When we are together, I wish our conversation was more meaningful."

Time and *talk*—these were the two top issues on the minds of the wives of our men.

Perhaps the biggest deposit of all, what can most signal that you want to love your wife sacrificially, that you want to make her your top priority after God, is to just say, "I want to be my wife's best friend."

This happened for me at the thirteen-year mark of marriage. We had two awesome kids, a beautiful home, the dream job. Everything should have been great. But it wasn't. Here's what was confusing. We had a good marriage. But because it wasn't a bad marriage, I had lulled myself into thinking it was better than it really was. We were just drifting.

One day, I remember praying, "God, what has happened here? I can remember when I first saw that woman walking down the street and my heart would thump and I would feel like it was going to pound out of my chest. I remember how my knees would wobble and my legs would feel like they were going to buckle.

"God," I said, "I want that back! I want to have that feeling back again. What can I do?"

God spoke to me. Over the next few days the thought formed, *Why don't you make Patsy your best friend?*

I said, "God, I'll do that! But, God, I have a problem. I have no idea *how* to do that."

After praying for a couple more weeks, the idea came to me one day:

After the children leave the dinner table and go off to do home-work, why don't you hang around at the dinner table for about twenty minutes and just talk. Listen without giving an overly quick reply. Just talk, but not about balancing the family checkbook, not doing family business, but just really getting to know or re-know this fragile flower that has been entrusted to you, a woman who wants intimacy, who is vulnerable with a desire for you. Why don't you just spend that time with her?

And that's what I did, without mentioning why. I started hanging around the table for an extra twenty minutes after dinner.

You know what? She stayed.

A few months later, I came home from work one day and she had bought me a present—a little plaque. I have it on my desk. I'm looking at it right now. It says, "Happiness is being married to your best friend."

A CALL TO ACTION

Men, the party will be over soon. The crepe paper will be drooping down low. The lights will be dimmed. Your kids will be grown and gone. Your friends will have moved to Florida or Arizona. There will only be two rocking chairs sitting side by side.

Doesn't it make sense to invest today in the woman who's going to be sitting next to you then? Which of the ideas we've highlighted—the 70 percent mind-set, praying for and with your wife, the emotional bank account, and making her your best friend—are ideas you want to make your call to action? Remember, you really are the only two people who are in this together.

Our dearest Father, thank you for this grand topic that really towers above all other aspects of our lives. Lord, some of us just needed to be reminded of something we're already doing. Others of us needed to be reminded to make an adjustment or correction. For some of us, this was good input for an upcoming or future marriage. Whatever the case, God, we do pray that after you, but before anyone or anything else, we each would make our wives our top priority. We pray this, Jesus, in your name. Amen.

And now, please answer the questions.

Reflection and Small Group Discussion Questions

1. Are you married? If not, do you want to be married? Either way, what do you think you can get from being married that you can get no other way? *a honest evaluation of myself - behavior*

2. The Scriptures in this chapter are the irreducible minimums that summarize what the Bible says about marriage. Which one verse has most impacted you, and why?

3. The big idea for this chapter is, "Most marriage problems would disappear if we would simply speak to our wives with the same kindness, courtesy, forethought, and respect with which we speak to our coworkers." First, do you think this is a good credo for you to adopt personally, and why? Second, what are two or three things you could do over the next few days that would send your wife or future wife the message that she really is your top priority after God—maybe it's one of the practical ideas in this chapter?

FIVE

CHILDREN

A Dad Who Really
Makes a Difference

Folly is bound up in the heart of a child.

PROVERBS 22:15

"Yes, I love you, and no, you
can't have your own way."

When my dad was two years old, the youngest of four children, his father abandoned the family. My dad's single mom did they best she could, but they were extremely poor.

To help support the family, my father started working when he was six years old. He had two jobs. Every day he and his older brother, Harry, would get up at 3:00 a.m. and work on a bread truck. Then they delivered newspapers before school.

When Dad became a man, he had a decision to make. Would he follow in his father's footsteps or break the cycle? You can imagine how happy I am that my dad wanted to be a cycle breaker. The legacy of some men is how far they go, but my dad's legacy can only be understood by looking at how far he came.

The impact of a father is undeniable. I am who I am today largely because my dad decided *not* to be the man his father was. I will always be so grateful. Thank you, Dad.

THE UN-DISCIPLED DAD

But my father had a problem. He never felt the scratch of his father's whiskers. He never heard the soothing sound of his father's voice reading him a bedtime story. He never had his father tousle his hair or wrestle him to the ground. He never tossed a ball with his dad in the backyard. He never smelled his father's work clothes. He never heard a truck door slam at the end of the day, signaling that his father was about to reenter the family orbit. He never heard his father say, "Son, I love you," or "Son, I'm proud of you."

In other words, what it meant to be a father was completely un-exampled to him. As a result, he had to *guess* at how to be a father to my three younger brothers and me.

Fathering wasn't a problem for my dad during the preteen years. But he was completely caught off guard by how rebellious, angry, and foolish I became as a teenager. I fell in with the party crowd, drank too much, started skipping school, and got into fistfights—a lot of fights.

Why did I become like that? Proverbs 22:15 says, "Folly is bound up in the heart of a child, but the rod of discipline will drive it far away."

Every child starts out foolish. In my case, my dad had no fathering model for discipline, instruction, and correction to fall back on. It wasn't his fault. As the saying goes, "You can't give what you didn't get." You see, he simply wasn't equipped to father the folly bound up in the heart of his child.

He had no training, no instruction, no discipleship. He was never invited to attend a parenting class or read a book like this. He didn't have a men's group or a couples' group where he could get advice about how to handle my running away from home, having three encounters with law enforcement for drinking too much, and always getting into fights.

As a result, I ended up with a huge chip on my shoulder. And I dared anyone to try to knock it off. By the middle of my senior year, I was so far off the rails that I quit high school. My dad wasn't going to let me hang around the house, so he drove me to the US Army enlistment office.

That turned out to be a great move, because in addition to protecting America's freedom, the US Army has an impeccably successful system to knock chips off the shoulders of foolish young men.

In my case, the system was spearheaded by a ferocious drill

sergeant who started each day by turning on every light in the barracks at 5:00 a.m. Then he'd lean down and put his grill six inches from my face and revel in screaming at the top of his lungs, "Get out of that bunk, you lazy piece of @$%#! Put on those combat boots, soldier! We're going for a five-mile run before breakfast."

The Army was good for me. I knew my dad loved me. However, it was the Army, through its discipline, that knocked the folly out of me.

Had the Army not dispensed the discipline that my father was not trained to give me, that chip on my shoulder could easily have ruined my life. Proverbs 19:3 tells us, "A person's own folly leads to their ruin, yet their heart rages against the LORD."

Of course, there are a lot of angry men out there who still have those chips on their shoulders. Their hearts are full of rage. If you are one of those men, I would encourage you to not judge your father more harshly than he deserves. Most dads really want the best for their children, even those not equipped to give it. Sure, they made mistakes. You'll make them too with your children. Forgive your father. And be sure to ask him to forgive you too, if possible. Many of us have been a lot more severe with our dads than they deserve.

With that said, every Christian father wants his children to grow up to love God and to love others. The purpose of this chapter is to give you the basic training on how to father your children in a way that will really make a difference for them.

WHAT OUR KIDS REALLY NEED

The challenging mission of a Christian father is to provide enough structure to drive out folly, while never letting your children have any reason to doubt that you unconditionally love and accept them.

When our own children were barely out of diapers, my wife and I attended a parenting seminar where counselor and author Larry Crabb was the speaker. He offered a simple, practical formula for correcting folly: "Yes, I love you, and no, you can't have your own way."

Virtually every parenting error you can think of will be the result of getting one or both statements out of kilter:

The *Authoritarian* Father: "No, I don't love you, and no, you can't have your own way."

The *Permissive* Father: "Yes, I love you, and yes, you can have your own way."

The *Disconnected* Father: "No, I don't love you, and yes, you can have your own way."

The *Encouraging* Father: "Yes, I love you, and no, you can't have your own way."

"Yes, I love you, and no, you can't have your own way" is the big idea that can guide you to the right balance of structure and discipline you will need to drive out folly, while at the same time making sure your children never doubt your love.

YOUR PARENTING STYLE

One of our Bible study leaders told me, "No matter what I did, I just could never make my dad happy." Did your father make you feel unconditionally loved and accepted? You know how pleasant or painful that feels—even now.

Every father wants to know, "What does it mean to be too strict? If I am too strict, what will happen? What does it mean to be not strict enough? If I am too permissive, what will happen?"

When it comes to providing structure, there are two possible errors. The first error is *too much structure*. For example, a woman raged against God to her dying breath because she grew up in a "Christian" home where she wasn't allowed to wear makeup, listen to music, or go to parties. Too much structure can quickly devolve into legalism.

The second and opposite error is *not enough structure*. My wife said to me one day, "I think your parents gave you too much say." By not having clearly marked boundaries, many parents unwittingly create fear in their children by not giving them the safety of enough structure.

Focus on the Family founder James Dobson popularized a story about some elementary school children playing happily inside a fenced schoolyard. A few psychologists decided the fence created an artificial boundary that inhibited the children from flourishing. They successfully lobbied their case and the fence was removed. Immediately, the children huddled in a little mass in the center of the playground. Not knowing where the boundaries were had destroyed their confidence.

What's the right balance? As David Delk and I wrote in *The Dad in the Mirror*, there are basically two fathering styles: fathering for performance *and* fathering the heart.[1]

Many dads father for performance. They focus on external behavior and try to get their children to "do the right things." They exasperate their children. Scripture warns, "Fathers, do not exasperate your children; instead, bring them up in the training and instruction of the Lord" (Ephesians 6:4).

Fathering the heart is the approach the Bible recommends. Fathering the heart means to look not only at the behavior but also at the reasons *beneath* the behavior: "For the mouth speaks what the heart is full of," Jesus said (Matthew 12:34).

That's why we told our kids they could experiment with anything as long as it wasn't harmful or permanent. We were more interested in what was going on in their hearts than their behavior. Our son decided he wanted to grow his hair long. He got the nickname "the mop" around school. Then he decided he wanted to bleach his hair. We said okay. It turned orange, so he was "the orange mop" for about a year.

You can raise your children under grace or law, but grace is better. If you raise your children with too much structure, they're very likely to reject what you've tried to teach them once they're old enough to be on their own.

Here's a simple rule to help you balance structure: *Do not allow what God prohibits, and do not prohibit what God allows.*

I know that every Christian dad *wants* to father the heart. But what can you do *practically* to make sure your children really and truly believe you love them unconditionally?

Practical Ideas

You can give your children what they need by loving their mother, discipling your children, spending time with your kids, praying for them, and encouraging them with words. Let's spend the rest of this chapter exploring some of the most practical ways you can make that happen.

Love Their Mother

As newlyweds, my wife and I attended a marriage encounter weekend led by a cussing, smoking priest, which I thought was pretty funny since he wasn't married. But as it turned out, he was brilliant. He quoted Theodore Hesburgh, former president of the University of Notre Dame, who said, "The most important thing a father can do for his children is to love their mother."

This idea is at the heart of family systems theory.[2] Family counselors know if they successfully treat a child but return that child to an otherwise unchanged family system, the probability is statistically much higher that the child will return to his or her previous dysfunction.

It turns out the best predictor of healthy children is a healthy marriage. It's overstating the case to make a point, but basically, if you get your marriage right, you will get your family right too. The single most practical thing a dad can do to make a difference with his children is to really love their mom.

Disciple Your Children

Most of us have heard (and cling to) the axiom of Proverbs 22:6: "Train up a child in the way they should go, and when they are old, they will not turn from it" (my paraphrase).

There's a cluster of words—*train, disciple, discipline, instruct, teach, equip*—that describe a parent's responsibility for the transfer of spiritual, moral, and practical knowledge. It's what Jesus called "making disciples," and it's beautifully captured in this psalm:

> My people, hear my teaching;
>> listen to the words of my mouth.
> I will open my mouth with a parable;
>> I will utter hidden things, things from of old—
> things we have heard and known,
>> things our ancestors have told us.
> We will not hide them from their descendants;
>> *we will tell the next generation*
> *the praiseworthy deeds of the Lord,*
>> *his power, and the wonders he has done.*
> He decreed statutes for Jacob
>> and established the law in Israel,
> *which he commanded our ancestors*
>> *to teach their children,*
> *so the next generation would know them,*
>> *even the children yet to be born,*
>> *and they in turn would tell their children.*

Then they would put their trust in God
    and would not forget his deeds
    but would keep his commands.
                            Psalm 78:1–7, emphasis added

As you can see, making disciples of our children is primarily the responsibility of the parents. Youth pastors can assist us, but discipleship starts at home. We said in the chapter on spiritual growth that a disciple is

- *called* to live "in" Christ (salvation, abiding with him)
- *equipped* to live "like" Christ (growth, transformation)
- *sent* to live "for" Christ (love and deeds)

This three-part definition is a great framework for discipling your kids.

First, make sure your children hear on a regular basis *about the gospel of Jesus that offers salvation.* At the appropriate time, ask them if they would like to receive Jesus. It goes without saying, but every Christian parent wants their children to understand, see in action, and embrace the gospel of Jesus. Just be sure you don't delegate this task to anyone else. Sure, your church can help you, but it's just too important to not oversee for yourself!

Second, show them by your example and through instruction from you and others how Jesus lived his life. Encourage them to trust Jesus and live by his example in the details of life.

Third, show your children what it looks like to be a man or woman of God in a world that has grown weary of Christian talky-talk and yearns to see authentic examples of Christianity.

For the rest of this chapter, I've assembled the best ideas for you from all my books, especially *The Dad in the Mirror* and *Man Alive.*

Practically speaking, you can disciple your children by leading them in family devotions, encouraging personal devotions, and taking them to church.

Lead Family Devotions. There's just something about putting your children into the Scriptures. During the school year, take five minutes before school three or four mornings a week. Share a relevant story from current events or a pithy quote, read a Bible verse, and then relate them together.

Close with a short time of prayer. Ask, "Who do you know who needs prayer today?" That will inspire your children to put some thought into their prayers instead of simply praying, "Lord, let us have a good day." Tell your children they can give the devotion any day they have something special to share.

In my case, I started running the devotions too long, which made our kids late for school. My wife suggested setting a timer. That allowed our children to relax and not worry they would be late for school. Take summers off because sleep schedules are different.

Pay Your Children for Personal Devotions. Pay your children to establish the habit of regular devotions. A range of five to fifteen minutes per day is good. Encourage them to use a reader-friendly version of the Bible. Or let them use a youth devotional if that suits them better.

Here's how we did it. We told our children, "If you will do a daily devotion for at least twenty-five days each month, we'll pay for you to buy some music."

They said, "That's nice, Dad."

"That's not all," we added. "In addition, if you do your devotions at least twenty-five days each month for ten out of twelve months, we'll pay you $____. You can miss any two months and still get paid." Their eyes popped open.

"But that's not all. If you will do your devotions all twelve months in a row, we'll double the amount and pay you $____. And you still only have to do twenty-five days a month. And if you miss a day, you can make it up."

I left out the amounts we paid, because the amounts can vary from $100, or even less, to several hundred dollars, depending on your life situation. What really matters is that the amount fits your budget and feels significant to your children.

They each taped a calendar to their bathroom mirror and marked a big "x" through each date when they completed a devotion. We used the honor system.

You may be thinking to yourself, *That sounds like a bribe.* Here's what I can tell you: our kids did regular devotions all through high school; none of their friends did; and one year they said, "Mom and Dad, you don't have to pay us anymore. We're going to be doing this anyway." You will feel a high level of satisfaction when you see your children dig into the Scriptures for themselves.

Take Your Children to Church. We took our children to church because that was part of what it meant to be a Morley. Many parents wonder, *Should we force our children to go to church if they don't want to go?* This can best be answered by another question: *Should we force our children to go to school if they don't want to go?*

Taking preteens to church works easily, but sometimes teens will tell you they're too tired to go to church. If that becomes a problem, transfer the responsibility for being in church to your children. Tell them, "If you don't make it to church that's fine, but then you can't go out next Saturday night."

In our family, that was tested—once. When we followed through with the promised consequence, it never happened again. We followed the rule, "Yes, I love you, and no, you can't have your own way."

Spend Time with Your Kids

Jason said, "I always wanted to be able to provide for my family, so I started a company—a trucking company, one truck. Short hauls around town. I'm the only employee. I did it because I really wanted to provide a better life for my family. My family was my top priority, and so I started the business with the goal of making a better life for my family.

"But then business picked up. Before I knew it, I was leaving home before sunrise and getting home at night after dark." He said, "One night, I came home. My wife met me at the door and said that when she was putting our three-and-a-half-year-old son Shawn to bed that night, he sat up in bed and asked, 'Mommy, where does Daddy live?'"

At first he laughed it off. But as he thought about it, he said, "Oh my gosh. I've gotten the ends and the means mixed up! This business was going to be the means for me to meet the end of providing for my family. But instead, my family has become the means to reach the end of building the business. How did this happen?"

Jason decided to make a change and lead a more balanced life. It took him two years to make it right.

A chief responsibility of being a father is time. If you don't have enough time for your children, you can be 100 percent certain that you're not following God's will for your life.

Here are several practical ways you can spend more time with your children: by setting work boundaries, giving them time in the way they want to receive it, dating them when they're teens, and eating dinner together.

Set Work/Family Boundaries. Not everybody can set their own hours, but if you can, this is a great area where you can be intentional. I could, so I decided not to work past 6:00 p.m. on weekdays, not work on weekends, and not take work home. This was tough, because I love to work.

Here's how I disciplined myself. Every day on the way home, I would drive over a creek about three minutes from our home. Before I got to the bridge, I would allow myself to think about work. But when I reached that bridge, I would put everything into an imaginary briefcase, toss it over the wall, and mentally see it splash into the creek. That gave me three good minutes to prepare for reentry into the world of my wife and kids.

You're going to set some boundaries for your kids. Set some boundaries for yourself too—some work boundaries—if you can. Or find a different job that allows you to give time to whom time is due.

Give Kids Time How They Want It. The best way to give time to your kids is in the way they want to receive it. Once I arrived home, I would take fifteen minutes to change clothes, wash the grease off my face, and look at the mail before we ate dinner as a family, and then also spend twenty minutes with Patsy after dinner to see what kind of day she was having. After that, I spent 100 percent of my time with our children until they went to bed.

When our children were young, we played board games. We played endless repetitions of *Chutes and Ladders* and mind-numbing rounds of *Candyland*—both of which require the IQ of an earthworm. Later, when they graduated to team sports and music lessons, their mother and I attended all their events.

So, if your kids like to play board games, play board games. If your kids like to go to movies, go to movies. If your kids like ice cream or gelato places, go for it. If they like to have books read to them, read them books. If they want to play video games with you, play video games with them.

Dating Your Teens. Here's a thought especially for young dads. You may think you have your kids for eighteen years, and in one sense, you do. And when your children are under the age of twelve, they will love playing with their dad. But around twelve years of age, their friends become very important, so you will need to get creative.

When our children started wanting to hang out with their friends more than their parents, I started dating them. We have two children, so each Tuesday I took one child to dinner, the next week the other one. We always topped it off with go-carts, a trip to the shopping mall, ice cream, or sometimes a movie. They genuinely looked forward to the special time with Dad.

Allowing for holidays and vacations, I knew through their teen years that I was going to have about twenty evenings a year with each child. In hindsight, the vast majority of the one-on-one conversations we've ever had were on those date nights. I shudder to think of how little "just the two of us" conversation we would have had otherwise!

Eat Dinner Together. There's some research suggesting that eating dinner together is a main way family values are passed from one generation to the next. We always ate dinner together as a family. When our children were teens, I sometimes had to twist arms with my kids and their coaches. There were compromises. Sometimes we had to eat early. Sometimes we had to eat late. Sometimes we had to eat at Burger King.

Be sure to set a good discipleship example and always say a prayer before you start your meal. Say grace in words that draw attention to the connection between the food and God's grace to provide it. This will help instill a spirit of gratitude.

Pray for Your Children

You already know this, but you and your wife (and possibly your parents) are probably the only people in the whole world who would be willing to pray for your children on a regular basis. Pray for your children every day. Write down the areas you're praying for. You can develop your own list or adapt my list from *The Man in the Mirror*:

- a saving faith (thanksgiving if already Christian)
- a growing faith
- an independent faith (as they grow up)
- their strength and health in mind, body, and spirit
- a sense of destiny (purpose)
- a desire for integrity
- a call to excellence
- an understanding of the ministry God has for them
- my commitment to set aside times to spend with them
- a thirst to acquire wisdom
- protection from drugs, alcohol, and premarital sex
- the mate God has for them (alive somewhere, needing prayer)
- a passion to glorify the Lord in everything[3]

Encourage Your Children with Words

There are two statements that every child longs to hear—repeatedly: "I love you" and "I'm proud of you."

Our son was playing point guard in a high school basketball game. It was the first time my father and mother had seen him play. They were sandwiched between my wife and me, with my mother to my immediate left. I was telling her, "We are just so proud of John for the diligence that he's shown, for being a team player, the leadership qualities he's developing, his industry, and all of the fine things that are happening. We're just so proud of him."

At that point, my mother who was staring into the distance wistfully said to no one in particular, "You know, when our four boys were growing up, I don't think we told them often enough that we were proud of them."

I was thinking, *Hey, Mom, I'm one of those four boys. You don't have to talk in the third person. I'm sitting right here!*

And then my brain exploded and split in two. One half of my brain wanted to scream at the top of my lungs, *That's right! You didn't do that! Why didn't you do that? You could've done that. It would've been so easy to do that! Just to let us know that you were proud of us! Why didn't you do that?*

And then the other half of my brain wanted to scream the second thought: *It's not too late, Mom! It's not too late. You can do it now. You can tell me now!*

It would've been so easy for them to do that, but of course, they didn't know how because they'd never been trained like I'm training you to disciple your kids. So there I sat, in my late thirties, aching, yearning, longing for my mom to say that she was proud of me.

In fact, it was not until I was forty-seven years of age that I knew for sure my dad was proud of me. I figured he was, but that's not the same as hearing it. Here's how it happened.

When I was thirty-five, I longed to restore a relationship with my dad—the one I had wrecked as a teen when I dropped out of school. I invited my dad to lunch on his birthday. He accepted, and it became an annual tradition.

When I was forty-seven, I wrote on his birthday card, "Dad, I sure hope you're proud of me." I watched him across the table as he read the card and, without looking up, said, "Well, you know I am." That's all I ever got! But it was electricity. It unchained something inside me.

Men, in the name of Jesus, I adjure you, tell your children every day, "I love you!" and "I'm proud of you!" Every day. At every opportunity. Be repetitious. Tell your children, "I love you" and "I'm proud of you." Over and over again.

And if your kids are already grown? Call them today—don't merely text or email—and tell them how much you love them and how proud you are of them!

This is not without biblical precedent. When the Father came in the form of the Holy Spirit at the baptism of Jesus (Matthew 3:13–17) and also at the transfiguration (Matthew 17:1–8), what did he say? "This is my Son, whom I love." *I love you!* "With him I am well pleased." *I'm proud of you!*

So encourage your children with words. Encouraging words are the food of the heart, and every heart is a hungry heart.

MAKE YOUR FAMILY YOUR #1 MINISTRY

No one else cares about your family like you do. No one else can, or should, take responsibility to disciple your family. That one's on you.

Your family is your most important small group, prayer group, fellowship group, discipleship group, and ministry. Until you get your family right, you really shouldn't be doing ministry anywhere else.

But you have to be strong, and you have to set boundaries, because our children really do have folly bound up in their hearts.

Remember, the antidote to folly is unconditional love and structure. You can deliver the antidote by sticking to the big idea for this chapter: "Yes, I love you, and no, you can't have your own way."

To help you be that dad who makes a difference, we've looked at many practical ideas that can help you. As we end, please take a moment and check off the ideas that interest you, whether that's now or later when you start a family—and let that be your call to action for this chapter.

_____ I will love their mother well.

_____ I will disciple my children.

_____ I will lead family devotions.

_____ I will pay my children for personal devotions.

_____ I will take my children to church.

_____ I will spend time with my kids.

_____ I will set work/family boundaries.

_____ I will give my kids time the way they want to receive it.

_____ I will date my teens.

_____ We will eat dinner together.

_____ I will regularly pray for my children.

_____ I will encourage my children with words.

_____ I will tell my children often, "I love you" and "I'm proud of you."

I pray the lessons in this chapter will bring you success on your mission. Next, why do you think friendships are so important to men? Pray the prayer, answer the questions, turn the page, and let's find out!

Our dearest Father, we come humbly looking for grace, mercy, and forgiveness. We're coming before you because we want to be all that you have created us to be in this area of being fathers. Lord, help us to be the fathers that our children need. Help us disciple into their lives what they need to become adults who don't have folly bound up in their hearts. Give us wisdom to help our children walk in the freedom of the gospel of our Lord and Savior, Jesus Christ, in whose name we make this prayer. Amen.

Reflection and Small Group Discussion Questions

1. As a child, did you feel unconditionally loved and accepted by your father, and why or why not? How much structure did your father provide—too much, too little, or just about right? How has that affected your own parenting style?

2. The challenging mission of a Christian father is to provide enough structure to drive out folly while never giving your children reason to doubt that you unconditionally love and accept them. Why is that challenging? How could the big idea for this chapter—"Yes, I love you, and no, you can't have your own way"—help you make a difference?

3. Do you think your children feel unconditionally loved and accepted by you, and why or why not? What has been covered in this chapter that gives you hope? Which of the practical ideas did you check off as your call to action, and why?

SIX

FRIENDSHIPS

Finding and Keeping
Godly Friends

There is a friend who sticks closer than a brother.

PROVERBS 18:24

What's really going to help you long-term is to find a friend or two, or join a small group, and live life together with a few brothers with whom you can process what comes your way.

My wife and I pulled up to a stoplight next to a Lamborghini. I cracked the window to let in the throaty rumble from the exhaust pipes of the 700+ horsepower engine. The light turned green, and the driver lit it up.

I said with no small amount of admiration, "Wow! Can you believe that?"

My wife turned to me and said, "No, I can't believe that either. That's just so dangerous."

Our wives can be our best friends, but there's a reason women and men separate into two groups at the Labor Day picnic.

Male friendship was a hot topic with the storyboard group for this book. Steve captured the spirit of the men with his questions, "How do I develop meaningful friendships with other men when we are all very busy? And without taking time away from family? How do I find men who are genuinely open to friendship? The men I know don't seem interested."

In this chapter, we're going to see the integral role that friendships play in God's plan for manhood, and we'll look at the practical aspects of how to start and maintain authentic friendships. But first let's look at the problem addressed by friendship.

THE PROBLEM

The fallen world is a never-sleeping juggernaut that relentlessly crushes everything in its path without pity—our dreams, our plans, and our relationships. We fight back, but eventually the accumulation of thousands of unfair and unjust criticisms, insults, accusations, rejections, slights, innuendos, disrespect, gossip, offenses, bullying, getting overlooked, feeling kicked to the curb, being denied access, getting ambushed, being undervalued, and getting thrown under the bus takes a toll.

We tire of the snarky, lusty, rude, crude, coarse, envious, jealous, arrogant, and pretentious comments people make. The disgraceful, greedy, unethical, and illegal behavior of others staggers our sensibilities. The endless onslaught of trials, temptations, sins, errors in judgment, and failure wears us down. We're dulled by the wicked thoughts of our own felonious hearts. We are riddled by shame and guilt for all the ways we have let others down.

It adds up. At a point, without some outside help, it all just gets to be too much. We despair over the evil we see that people are capable of inflicting on each other. Our faith in humanity is gutted. We become fragile. Prickly. Easily offended. Lose our resilience. Hope fades away. Bitterness crushes what little happiness our hearts were holding on to. Our wills get broken. We are prone to withdraw, even if we keep up our daily routines. Despair sets in. We isolate ourselves from friends.

Because I work with men as a vocation, I often meet men when this despair and isolation have taken over. As I wrote in *Man Alive*, when men try to express their inner aches and pains—what's really bothering them—they invariably mention one or more of seven troubling symptoms:

- I just feel like I'm in this all alone.
- I don't feel like God cares about me *personally*—not really.
- I don't feel like my life has a purpose. It seems random.
- I have a lot of destructive behaviors that keep dragging me down.
- My soul feels dry.
- My most important relationships are not working.

- I don't feel like I'm doing anything that will make a difference and leave the world a better place.[1]

I often receive an email or phone call from men at just this point. After listening, the first thing I always ask is, "Do you have a best friend, or are you part of a small group?"

In 100 percent of the cases, the answer is, "No, why do you ask?" Often men will add, "I used to meet with a guy, but we stopped," or "I used to be part of a small group, but I haven't been going for a while."

Usually I can help men with the issue at hand, but then I urge them—and this is the big idea for this chapter—"What's really going to help you long-term is to find a friend or two, or join a small group, and live life together with a few brothers with whom you can process what comes your way."

A man is never more weak and vulnerable than when he doesn't have a friend or two.

HOW FRIENDSHIP IS CENTRAL TO THE GOSPEL

We are made for relationships. A godly friendship can change everything. There is a peculiar math to friendship: shared joys are doubled, and shared sorrows are cut in half.

Friendship is a central theme of Jesus' life and teaching. He tells us to encourage each other: "My command is this: Love each other as I have loved you. Greater love has no one than this: to lay down one's life for one's friends" (John 15:12–13).

In fact, loving one another is the evidence of our identity as disciples: "By this everyone will know that you are my disciples, if you love one another" (John 13:35)

When the world beats you down, Jesus has a cure for that: godly friends. When Jesus came to the tomb of his friend, Lazarus, he was deeply moved. After he had the stone that sealed the tomb taken away, Jesus prayed. And after he prayed, "Jesus called in a loud voice, 'Lazarus, come out!' The dead man came out, his hands and feet wrapped with strips of linen, and a cloth around his face. Jesus said to them, "Take off the grave clothes and let him go" (John 11:43–44).

Jesus brought Lazarus back to life, but when Lazarus came out of the tomb, he was still bound in grave clothes. Instead of removing them himself—which he could have easily done, Jesus told the *other* friends of Lazarus, "You help him take off the grave clothes and finish setting him free."

The Lazarus story is a real story about a real man. But it is also a metaphor for a man who has been beaten down by the world. The juggernaut has rolled over him and crushed his dreams, hopes, and relationships. He is overwhelmed. Withdrawn. Isolated. Alone. Spiritually dead.

Or perhaps worse, like the zoo lion in this book's prologue, he is a man who has accepted his situation.

The only *real* hope for such a man is that Jesus Christ, the friend of sinners, will be his friend and raise him from the dead and arrange for some friends to remove his grave clothes.

Friends are not God's backup plan. Friends are God's plan A. Jesus will resurrect a man from the dead, but then he gives the joy, privilege, and responsibility of fully setting the man free to his friends.

Clark Miller, one of the regional directors at our ministry, Man in the Mirror, was meeting with a small group of men. During a weekly meeting to discuss destructive behaviors, he divided them into groups of three or four men and encouraged them to open up about the baggage holding them back. "What's the thing that's been eating you up that you haven't been able to share with a real friend? We've been together as a group for a long time, so let's open up with each other a little bit." Or, in so many words, help take off each other's grave clothes.

An older man who never said much opened up for the very first time. He said, "My younger sister was raped when she was only five years old." He went on to explain that as her older brother, he had always in some ways felt responsible for what happened. He concluded, "This is the first time in sixty-five years I have ever talked about it."

Suddenly, something lifted. The grave clothes came off. He was set free because the other brothers were kind and really cared. Clark said, "Since that meeting his entire persona changed. He has been dramatically freed, and he has been touched. He has been able to talk through this in a way that has brought healing."

We've already established that the world is going to beat you down. The only question is whether you will face that alone.

DO YOU HAVE A FRIEND OR TWO LIKE THIS?

What can you get from a friend that you can get no other way? Look at how the Bible describes the benefits of friendship, but also notice why we need friends in the first place.

- *Godly friends will make you stronger.* "Two are better than one, because they have a good return for their labor: If either of them falls down, one can help the other up. But pity anyone who falls down and has no one to help them up. Also, if two lie down together, they will keep warm. But how can one keep warm alone? Though one may be overpowered, two can defend themselves. A cord of three strands is not quickly broken" (Ecclesiastes 4:9–12).

- *Godly friends love you no matter what.* "A friend loves at all times, and a brother is born for a time of adversity" (Proverb 17:17).
- *Godly friends are there for you when you need them.* "One who has unreliable friends soon comes to ruin, but there is a friend who sticks closer than a brother" (Proverbs 18:24).
- *Godly friends are faithful and trustworthy.* "Many claim to have unfailing love, but a faithful person who can find?" (Proverbs 20:6).
- *Godly friends hold each other accountable.* "Wounds from a friend can be trusted, but an enemy multiplies kisses" (Proverbs 27:6).
- *Godly friends offer each other honest advice.* "The pleasantness of a friend springs from their heartfelt advice" (Proverbs 27:9.)
- *Godly friends disciple each other.* "As iron sharpens iron, so one person sharpens another" (Proverbs 27:17).
- *Godly friends restore each other.* "Brothers and sisters, if someone is caught in a sin, you who live by the Spirit should restore that person gently. But watch yourselves, or you also may be tempted" (Galatians 6:1).
- *Godly friends carry each other's burdens.* "Carry each other's burdens, and in this way you will fulfill the law of Christ" (Galatians 6:2).

How about you? Do you have a friend or two like those described in these Scriptures? Friends who would do anything for you—the kind you can call at 2:00 a.m. and they will come running? Do you have a friend with whom you can share confidential thoughts? Do you have a friend who cares enough to call you on the carpet when you're out of line? Do you have a friend for discipleship, growth, accountability, and prayer? Do you have a friend who will listen, really listen, when you're weighed down by the world—or you've really messed up?

A true friend, a 2:00 a.m. friend, is somebody who will stick with you when you have to declare bankruptcy, go through a divorce, are in bondage to drugs or alcohol, have a moral failure, lose your job, or have to deal with a child who has gone off the path.

A few 2:00 a.m. friends can make up for a multitude of disappointments. Let's turn our attention to how you can find—and keep—a handful of these godly friends. Friendships can be enjoyed one-on-one or in small groups. Here are guides on how to start both.

One-on-One Friendships
How to Start a One-On-One Weekly Meeting

Let's say you think you and Daniel might click. How do you find out if he might develop into a friend? The first thing to know about starting a friendship is what *not* to do! *Don't violate the process of relationships.* Here's how *not* to go about it:

"Hey, Daniel, how's it going, my brother? Say, listen, I really like you a lot. I'm looking for a new friend, a close friend, a true friend—someone I would rush into a burning building to save and vice versa. Someone who can be a faithful friend, so we can be honest, open, authentic, vulnerable, and transparent with each other. We would share from the depths of our souls.

"So, Daniel, I was wondering if you would be that friend for me? We'll have each other's backs. It'll be great—friends for life. Jonathan and David stuff. We'll vacation with our families and spend time at each other's homes. We'll meet regularly and hold each other accountable. What do you think, Daniel, would you be my best friend?"

Obviously, that would completely freak Daniel out. There is

a process of relationships. The first time I saw my wife I didn't walk up to her and say, "Hey, Patsy, how are you doing? Would you like to get married?" Why? Because that would have obviously violated the process of relationships.

Instead, I said, "Hey, Patsy. I'm Pat. Would you like to go out Friday night?" I asked for a date—the appointment. She said no, but that's a story for a different book. Eventually I succeeded, and we clicked.

So, what would be an appropriate first step to find a new friend? It would be to see if you can get an appointment, "Hey, Daniel, you want to grab a cup of coffee sometime?"

When you have your coffee, it's normal to be sizing each other up. You want to know, *What is this man's character? What do I learn about him from what he says and how he lives his life?*

If you feel like coffee went well, you may say, "Hey, why don't we get together again in a couple weeks? I'd love to get to hear more about your family," or "Hey, we share a common interest in running. Why don't we go for a run sometime?"

If he says, "Sorry, I just don't have the margin right now," that's okay. You need to make an allowance that everyone is finite and has limited capacity. If for whatever reason he's not interested, go to the next guy and repeat the process.

You will need to be intentional and the one who initiates. Why? Because most men don't. Men are very passive when it comes to making friends. They just are! I've watched this now for my entire business and ministry careers. Men just don't take the initiative in friendships, generally speaking.

Suppose, however, he says, "Sure, let's go for a run." If after getting together a few times you feel like the two of you click, suggest you start meeting on a weekly basis. You could say something like, "Hey, I've been wanting to grow in my faith. What would you think about us starting to meet on a weekly basis?"

It doesn't have to be a long, drawn-out process. In fact, if you already know a man fairly well, you may even lead by asking him about a weekly get-together. That's what happened when I started meeting with Ken. Here's how it happened.

Tom Skinner was already one of my best friends. He was a speaker, and I heard him repeatedly say, "The most powerful force in the world is a relationship." He challenged a group of us one day, "If you want to change your city, you don't need to organize a citywide crusade. Instead, find one other man and become to that man what you would like your city to become. That will create a model so attractive that other people will be drawn to it."

That sank into the marrow of my soul, and I got excited. I started thinking about the men I knew, and Ken was one of the first who came to mind. We already went to church together, were in a couple's home group together, and enjoyed each other's company. So after returning home, I walked up to Ken at church and, after explaining how Tom had challenged us, said, "Ken, what would you think about us meeting once a week for fellowship and prayer? Who knows? Maybe we could become to each other what we would like this city to become?"

He said, "Sure, that sounds great!"

This is the same Ken in the story at the beginning of chapter 1. Literally everything I've ever done, whether in business or in ministry, I ran by Ken first. He was my friend, my confidant, and cheerleader. He would give me counsel. He would also tell me in a nice way when I had an idea that was really stupid. We prayed about everything.

Friendship in the Commonsense World

How many friendships you have is completely up to you, but as an example, for most of my adult life I've maintained two weekly meetings with individual friends and one men's group meeting that has met weekly, biweekly, and sometimes monthly.

If you're married, start with your wife—even though you both know there are "men things" and "women things" about which you'll each get more help from someone of the same gender. Next, develop friendships with your adult children if possible. Beyond family, any friendships of the "sharing what's really going on" kind must be same gender only.

How do you know if someone is really a 2:00 a.m. friend? Let's explore some of the things that would differentiate a 2:00 a.m. friend from your circle of friends. For starters, there's a huge difference between an acquaintance and a friend, and we all know what that is. There's also a profound difference between a close friend and a circle of friends. Most of us have a circle of friends that may include as many as fifty or more people. But there's no way you can remember much about fifty friends.

A 2:00 a.m. friend, on the other hand, knows the names of your children. You share meals together. Your families have met. You've been in each other's home. You meet or speak on a regular basis. Social media is a great way to keep up with your larger circle of friends and acquaintances, but your real friends want to look you in the eye and hang out.

Most friendships are situational and found "along the way." Male friendship leaves a unique heat signature, as most men organize getting together around tasks, not relationships. Unlike women, men need a "reason" to get together.

In practice, most of our relationships are situational. We tend to organize around a shared interest, such as children's activities, a Bible study at church, the gym, sports, or a hobby. Often, a man's closest friendships are with coworkers. Then one or two or three of those will extend beyond that into a long-term friendship.

Once Dr. Ben Carson spoke for us in Indianapolis, and we

rode together on a plane to the event. The topic of friendships came up, and he made the comment, "I really believe a man would be fortunate to have two or three really close friendships in his entire lifetime."

"What about you?" I asked.

He said, "I have a man who twenty years ago wrote me a letter and said he admired my work. He lived in Pittsburgh and said if I was ever there to come by and see him. So I went to Pittsburgh once, and I did. There was an instant connection! And so we have been friends for twenty years!"

I asked, "What does that look like?"

He said, "It means our families vacation together, and we have spent every Christmas together as families for twenty years."

The other way to make some 2:00 a.m. friends is to be in a men's small group. That's how it happened for Brian.

A Men's Small Group

Brian's church announced a men's group meeting. He didn't want to go, but he was so beat-up he didn't know where else to turn, so he decided to give it a try.

At the meeting, he stood off to the side, avoiding contact as much as possible. One of the men, Wayne, an area director for Man in the Mirror, noticed his fidgety body language and his eyes darting around the room.

He said to Brian, "You appear to be uncomfortable. May I ask what you're looking for? Maybe I can help."

Brian's answer was revealing. He said, "No, you can't help me. No one can. I'm trying to see if anyone else here is as screwed up as I am."

Wayne offered, "If you will be patient tonight, I think you're going to hear some stories that will amaze you and encourage you." That calmed Brian enough to take a seat.

The evening started with a video about the need for men to unpack their baggage. Next, a man got up and told his story about how God had reached into his broken life, renewed his faith, restored his marriage, and given him a new beginning. Several other men came during an open-mic time and shared similar stories.

Near the end of the meeting, Wayne looked over and saw Brian slip out of his seat and walk to the mic. Brian took a deep breath and held it, but no words came out. His shoulders started churning in a silent sob. Several men slipped out of their seats to surround him. One was praying. More men huddled. They put their hands on Brian's shoulders. Soon, all the men in the room were huddled around him.

Brian never spoke any words into the microphone that night. The next time Wayne saw Brian, the fidgeting was gone. His eyes had stopped darting around the room. Wayne asked him, "So what's different?"

Brian said. "My life is different. Jesus has forgiven me. I have found a band of brothers here at this church who didn't judge me and have accepted me. I can finally breathe."

Breathe. Finally. Because of Christ.

If you're not already in a small group, why not make getting in a group your call to action for this chapter?

You could, for example, join an existing small group. It can be men only, couples, mixed singles, or a combination. Groups which include women are good—I've been in several, but there's also an unparalleled bond that develops when men share just with men. So if you do have a group that includes women, separate the men and women once a month for guy talk.

What if you just can't find an existing group? Actually, that's highly probable. So here's a guide for you to start your own men's small group. And even if you're already in a group, the principles presented will be an excellent review to keep your existing group fresh and strong.

How to Start and Sustain a Weekly Men's Small Group

1. First, make a list of men you might like to have in your group. Figure you need to ask two or three men for every slot in your group. Pray over their names. Ask God to give you names you might not ordinarily think of.

2. Next, decide what kind of group you want to lead. You could wait and make a group decision, but it will likely fall apart. Leaders lead—and men like that. There are many different types of small groups, but most will be some combination of the following:

- *Bible Study and Discussion Groups* to read and discuss the Bible and/or books (six to twelve men—remember, twelve has been successfully used before!)
- *Service and Mission Teams* to do service and outreach projects (any number)
- *Support Groups* for prayer, accountability, fellowship, or specific issues like addictions (two to six men)
- *Sports Teams* (any number)

3. Decide when, where, and how often you want to meet. Friday mornings are good because most men try to be back in town by then, and it's often a catch-up day. If all your men are from the same church, you could meet on Sundays, on a weekday evening, or one morning during the week at the church. There are men's groups meeting in churches, cubicles, conference rooms, and restaurants all across America. A friend likes to say, "The largest men's Bible study in America is Panera Bread." Most groups tend to meet weekly, but many successful groups meet every other week or once a month.

4. Next, invite the men to an informational meeting to discuss the small group. Pick the time and place, and shoot for one hour but no more than ninety minutes. As you invite them,

- explain to the men what you are trying to accomplish and why
- don't ask men for a long-term commitment
- unless you feel strongly otherwise, tell them you will initially meet for four, six, or eight weeks (pick a number), and after that you will decide as a group where to go from there
- graciously let individuals decline your offer

THE FIRST MEETING

The first meeting is informational.

Have coffee and donuts/bagels or Cokes and cookies.

Meet for one hour but no more than ninety minutes.

Start on time and open with a brief prayer.

For five to ten minutes: Mention (again) your purpose for wanting to start a small group. Give the men an opportunity to comment on your proposed written "Purpose Statement" for the small group. Write it out beforehand and put "D-R-A-F-T" at the top. They will appreciate being asked and feel a stronger sense of ownership.

Next forty minutes: Depending on how many men you have, ask each man to take three to five minutes to share briefly where he is on his spiritual journey today and what he would like to "give and get" from the group.

Five minutes: Inspire them with your vision for the group. Encourage the men. Don't go too far too fast and violate the process of relationships. Be sensitive that most men will not jump in until they have tested the waters for a few weeks (or months).

Last five minutes: Pass out materials for the kick-off meeting, confirm the when and where, and close with a brief prayer.

How to Lead an Effective Discussion

Here are some hard-learned lessons about leading an effective discussion:

- "Air time for every man every week." Make sure men get to speak.
- You should draw out the quiet man without making him feel uncomfortable. Sense his pace. If he isn't ready to talk, don't try to force him. Privately ask the man who talks a lot to help you draw out the other men.
- Don't talk more than 25 percent of the time. If there is silence when you ask a question, don't try to fill the space.
- Ask open-ended questions, not ones that can be answered yes or no. Instead of asking, "Do you struggle with making good decisions?" ask "What kind of decisions do you find difficult, and why?"

Other Suggestions to Be Effective

Preferably call your men each week, but at least email or text them, to remind them about the meeting and express your genuine desire to see them. You want to make sure they feel you're more interested in them as a person than that you're just trying to put butts in seats. *This is a make-or-break point.*

Make it like family time, not work time (not as another duty to perform, but a place that will love and accept him no matter how bad he has screwed up). *This is also a make-or-break point.*

A small group is many things, including a hospital for men with broken wings. Make yours a *safe place* for men. Do not put pressure on men to conform to certain behaviors. Instead, show men Christ. Adopt the credo "long-term, low pressure."

Be sure to end on time—men appreciate punctuality.

After your group starts to gel, host a couples' social outing. Spend five hours per week on your group as your personal ministry (that's all-in—group time, phone calls/texts, personal visits, counseling men, etc.). Take each man out for coffee or a meal at least once a year if it's a long-term group.

If you are a marketplace small group, encourage your men to be actively involved in a disciple-making church. I've seen way too many men use our Bible study as a substitute for church, and their families have suffered greatly for it.

SELECTING SMALL GROUP RESOURCES

Bible Studies: If you have the time, aptitude, and interest, you can develop your own curriculum. If not, try the Man in the Mirror Weekly Bible Study. You can get it free online at www.mimbiblestudy.com, YouTube, and iTunes. Watch or listen to the message and then discuss the downloadable questions. We also have unedited transcripts if you want to teach the material yourself.

Book Studies: I am repeatedly amazed by how a man will get hold of a book, and then God will use that book to get hold of the man. I don't believe in Christian literature because I write books; I write books because I believe in Christian literature. Books change lives! One of the most effective ways to start a small group is to study a book with discussion questions for each chapter. Use this book. In the appendix, you can also find a list of some of my books that are suitable for groups, with brief descriptions.

Workbooks: You can find a plethora of small group resources at www.maninthemirror.org and from members of the National Coalition of Ministries to Men at www.ncmm.org.

Accountability Groups: See an example and order wallet-sized accountability cards at www.maninthemirror.org/accountability-cards.

WHAT MAKES A GROUP LAST?

Value is what makes a group last—more specifically, the perception of value. Every time a man shows up, he has decided not to do something else. Most men have many choices, so your small group has to meet the "real and felt needs test" or it won't last.

So what do men find valuable? Life can be brutal. Every day, men must manage their lives against the Fall. Because life is so hard, men need to be encouraged. They need a hug from God. They need the human touch. And this while wearing the skin of a loner.

The mega-answer? Care. Caring creates the value, that captures the momentum, that sustains the change. Men will come if they sense you really care about them. If not, they will soon drift away—but almost never tell you why.

You will know you have succeeded when you hear men saying things like, "I really feel like my group cares about me personally," "The leader makes sure I get a chance to air my thoughts," and "I cannot believe how my life is changing."

CONCLUSION

I pray you have or will find one, two, or three 2:00 a.m. friends. Because our big idea really is true: What's really going to help you long-term is to find a friend or two, or join a small group, and live life together with a few brothers with whom you can process what comes your way.

In the next chapter, we'll answer the question, "As a Christian man, how should I think about work?"

Our dearest Father in heaven, we come to you humbly. Lord, we don't want to be alone and we don't want to be lonely either. We know that you have created us for relationships. Lord, help us to take the initiative. Help us find those 2:00 a.m. friends who can help us overcome this multitude of disappointments that we all go through in life. And help us to be 2:00 a.m. friends to others. Lord, for those of us who already have friends like this, maybe today is the day when we just say to our friend, "Thank you so much for being my friend." In Jesus' name we pray. Amen!

Reflection and Small Group Discussion Questions

1. How many close friends do you have—the kind you can call at 2:00 a.m. and they will come running? Can you give an example?

2. We looked at a lot of Scripture in this chapter. What are the biblical ingredients of a true friendship that have been described? Which of those do you find most appealing, and why?

3. Are you happy with your close friendship situation, and why or why not? What, if anything, should be your call to action? What are some ideas you picked up, or have been reminded of, that can help you develop close friendships?

SEVEN

WORK

How Should I Think about My Work?

A person can do nothing better than to eat and drink and find satisfaction in their own toil. This too, I see, is from the hand of God, for without him, who can eat or find enjoyment?

ECCLESIASTES 2:24-25

There is no greater feeling than to believe, "This is what I'm supposed to be doing, right here, right now—even if it's hard."

One Friday afternoon, I picked up my car after it had been serviced at the dealership. As I checked out, I asked Christopher, the service representative with whom I've built a great rapport over the last three years, "How has your week been going?"

He sighed, shrugged his shoulders, and said, "Well, it's been going."

I said, "I'm sure it's challenging, but at least you have a job that will make a difference in the history of the world."

He didn't look at me like I was a nut. Actually, he seemed curious, so I continued. "All these people bring their cars to you for service so they can have reliable transportation to go to work where they will earn the money that pays for their groceries, car payments, rent, children's education, health care, and so much more. You are on the front line to make sure that happens.

"And then there are all the mothers who depend on you to make sure their cars work properly so they can safely drive their children to school, sporting events, and after-school activities.

"Imagine for a moment what would happen without you. People's cars would stop working; they would have no way to get them fixed; they wouldn't be able to go to work; their children would miss school; they wouldn't be able to pay their bills—it would be catastrophic."

Christopher said, "You know, I've never thought of it like that. I guess my work really does make a difference!"

I'm certain Christopher already felt like his work was worthwhile. But I also think he gained a fresh perspective about just how important his job is in the bigger scheme of things.

There is no greater feeling than to believe, "This is what I'm supposed to be doing, right here, right now—even if it's hard." That's the big idea for this chapter.

Do you have that feeling? Nothing is more normal than for you to find satisfaction in your work:

> This is what I have observed to be good: that it is appropriate for a person to eat, to drink and to find satisfaction in their toilsome labor under the sun during the few days of life God has given them—for this is their lot. Moreover, when God gives someone wealth and possessions, and the ability to enjoy them, to accept their lot and be happy in their toil—this is a gift of God.
>
> *Ecclesiastes 5:18–19*

And nothing is more excruciating than a job we don't like. My first "company" job, after mowing lawns and helping my dad for a couple of summers, was working in the produce department at Publix Super Markets during my senior year of high school. The problem was that I loved Publix (and still do), but I didn't like produce. Every day was a drudgery. It was agonizing to drag myself in to work because I did not enjoy it or find it satisfying.

In this chapter, we're going to explore where that feeling of satisfaction comes from, how you get it, and what you can do if you don't have it. We've already talked about balance. Now it's time to thrust ourselves into the hours we *do* work and free men up to do every task, however menial, as agents of Christ for the glory of God!

The twenty-four men who decided that "work" was a must issue to include in this book posed questions like, "I spend a lot of my life at work. How can I find ways to continue growing at work? How can I build a dynamic career that makes a difference in the world, while providing for my family?"

Is work something we do to earn money so that we can do what's really important, or is there intrinsic spiritual value in the work itself?

A THEOLOGY OF WORK

Not many men have a "theology" of work. That's unfortunate, since most of us will spend about half of our 112 waking hours each week at work if we include getting ready and drive times. Half of your life!

Every noble concept in the work world has been lifted straight out of the Bible, whether it's about excellence, integrity, vision, leadership, planning, execution, exceptional service, and so many other things. In fact, you could teach most of the Harvard Business School case study method right out of the book of Nehemiah. Yet many men would be hard-pressed to explain what Christians believe about work, so let's start there.

What should we think about work?

You were created to do real work that makes a real difference.

Whether you're bagging groceries, fixing a computer, pounding nails in a roof, practicing law, selling real estate, or whatever else—it's important. Work isn't merely something we endure to earn money to pay for the things we really want to do when we're not working.

There is intrinsic value in work. If you work at Home Depot, when you get a ladder and pull something off the upper shelf so that a housewife who can't reach it can get the product she wants, Christianity proclaims there's intrinsic value in that act.

Why do Christians believe this? It's because of a passage in the Old Testament known as "the cultural mandate." In addition to bringing the kingdom into our culture, God calls us to tend that culture as stewards of God's creation—this is "the cultural mandate." God has delegated dominion over creation to us as a sacred trust. Here's the key passage of Scripture:

> So God created mankind in his own image, in the image of God he created them; male and female he created them. God blessed them and said to them, "Be fruitful and increase in number; fill the earth and subdue it. Rule over the fish in the sea and the birds in the sky and over every living creature that moves on the ground."
>
> *Genesis 1:27–28*

Work is part of our DNA. God *designed* us to do good work on earth and charged us with tending all he's made. What an awesome privilege and responsibility!

Work is a calling for which you are ordained by God.

God doesn't just call us to salvation. He also calls us to work. God *ordained* Adam to agricultural work. He appointed him, giving him responsibilities and authority: "The LORD God took the man and put him in the Garden of Eden to work it and take care of it" (Genesis 2:15).

If you are an attorney, you are an ordained attorney. If you are a forest ranger, you are an ordained forest ranger. If you are a first responder, you are an ordained first responder. If you drive a bus, you are an ordained bus driver. If you are the service rep at an auto dealership, you are an ordained service rep.

Every vocation has dignity.

The world's first job was farming. There is dignity in every job, because every job makes a difference. Just ask anyone who has lived through a garbage strike.

Mike Rowe founded the television series *Dirty Jobs*. During an interview on one of the Sunday morning talk shows, he explained his big takeaway from doing the series: "For me, as a group, there was a level of job satisfaction that was undeniable and surprising. And it has to do with the ability to complete a task."

He also said, "In *Dirty Jobs*, the big lesson was there's an awful lot of people who are doing really important work who nobody really pays affirmative attention to."[1]

After that interview, I started watching the men around me doing dirty jobs. Our bug exterminator, Charles, is still going strong after forty years on the job. He loves his job and leaves a residue of joy, in addition to bug spray, once a month. He's providing a genuine and valuable service. If you've ever had a bug problem, you know this is work that really matters.

About the same time, our septic tank drain field had to be replaced. While the work only took a couple of days, the permitting process lasted two months. If you don't think that's a job that makes a difference, try living with an inoperable septic tank for two months! Those workers understood. From the very first day, all the men who worked at our home were enthusiastic and sincere about getting us back to normal. It brought them a great deal of personal satisfaction when they finally turned the last shovel of dirt over our repaired drain field.

Every vocation is sacred to the Lord.

The Bible makes no distinction between sacred and secular vocations. If you have a concordance in your Bible and look up all the references to the word *secular* in your Bible, how many do you think you would find? Zero, because the word *secular* does not appear in the Bible. There is no such thing as a secular job.

Every vocation is sacred. The Bible is dripping with the holiness and sanctity of vocation.

Work is hard because of the Fall.

I once asked Bill Bright—the founder of a large college ministry called Campus Crusade for Christ (now Cru)—who traveled constantly what percentage of his work was hard. He said, "Ninety percent of what I do is hard, but it's just what needs to be done." Oprah Winfrey once said, "People think I have this wonderful, glamorous life, and it is wonderful. But about 80 percent of it is just hard."

Work came first, and it was good. But because of the Fall, we must do our work while feeling the prick of thorns. We looked at this verse in the marriage chapter, but let's look at it again from the perspective of our work:

To Adam he said, "Because you listened to your wife and ate fruit from the tree about which I commanded you, 'You must not eat from it,'

"Cursed is the ground because of you;
   through painful toil you will eat food from it
   all the days of your life.
It will produce thorns and thistles for you,
   and you will eat the plants of the field.
By the sweat of your brow
   you will eat your food
until you return to the ground,
   since from it you were taken;
for dust you are
   and to dust you will return."

Genesis 3:17–19

Work is not just a platform for ministry; it *is* ministry.

Everything we do is for the glory of God. For example, whether you're an airline gate agent or a barista in a coffee bar, every customer is an occasion to demonstrate the character of Jesus Christ. If you are a manager, every conflict between two employees presents an opportunity to model the love of Christ. The apostle Paul wrote, "So whether you eat or drink or whatever you do, do it all for the glory of God" (1 Corinthians 10:31).

In other words, you don't just tolerate the work you're doing until the lunch break so you can do what's *really* important, like sharing your faith with a coworker over tacos. That's great, but if you haven't done your work well from 8:00 to 12:00, you're not really going to have credibility from 12:00 to 1:00.

Because there is intrinsic value in the work itself, it's not just a platform for ministry. The work itself *is* ministry. That's what produces the feeling, "This is what I'm supposed to be doing, right here, right now—even if it's hard."

Every interaction is an opportunity to bring glory and honor to Christ.

If you're a waiter and you have a couple sit at one of your tables, you don't know why they're there. They may be there for their anniversary, or it may be a weekly date night, or maybe they haven't gone out in twenty years. You don't know, but that couple sitting at your station is an opportunity for you to bring glory and honor to Jesus Christ by saying, with a smile, "Good evening. It's so nice to have you with us tonight. I'm really glad you're here." The same spirit applies if you are putting four new tires on a car or delivering an appliance.

God's plan is for us to do our work wholeheartedly as a representative of Jesus Christ:

Slaves [employees], obey your earthly masters in everything; and do it, not only when their eye is on you and to curry their favor, but with sincerity of heart and reverence for the Lord. Whatever you do, work at it with all your heart, as working for the Lord, not for human masters, since you know that you will receive an inheritance from the Lord as a reward. It is the Lord Christ you are serving.

Colossians 3:22–24,
bracketed comment added

It's okay, even desirable, to plunge yourself headlong into doing a great job. It is fitting to say, "How was your meal? May I get you some dessert tonight? It has been such a delight to have you as our guests this evening." You don't actually have to say the word "Jesus" to bring him glory and honor.

Provided you're not being asked to do something unethical or illegal, you should do what you're told or asked to do. Hopefully, you will be asked in a respectful way.

There is always a higher purpose to the work you're doing.

God is sovereignly orchestrating all human events, even the job we can't make sense of right now. He does so to bring us into right relationship with him and right relationship with each other.

If the Bible had a subtitle, a good one would be *Loving Father Relentlessly Pursues a Relationship with His Children*. Our jobs are a crucial venue for reconciliation with God and each other. These jobs we have—they are not random. God doesn't do random. He's using our work, and how we conduct our work, to both tend the culture (the cultural mandate) and build the kingdom (the Great Commission).

Doing your work well is a testimony in and of itself.

As already stated, work has intrinsic value. Nevertheless, work done well gives us a great opportunity to reflect favorably on the Christian faith: "Make it your ambition to lead a quiet life: You should mind your own business and work with your hands, just as we told you, so that your daily life may win the respect of outsiders and so that you will not be dependent on anybody" (1 Thessalonians 4:11–12).

It is good to enjoy your work and find it satisfying.

So I saw that there is nothing better for a person than to enjoy their work, because that is their lot. For who can bring them to see what will happen after them?

Ecclesiastes 3:22

This is what I have observed to be good: that it is appropriate for a person to eat, to drink and to find satisfaction in their toilsome labor under the sun during the few days of life God has given them—for this is their lot. Moreover, when God gives someone wealth and possessions, and the ability to enjoy them, to accept their lot and be happy in their toil—this is a gift of God.

Ecclesiastes 5:18–19

All men want to be happy. A man will feel most happy, most alive, and most useful when he is doing the kind of work he was created to do—even while feeling the prick of thorns.

We need to take work seriously.

I asked Jamie, a brilliant mid-thirties woman I work with in ministry to men, for her observations about work and men in her age group. What she said is too good not to just leave it in her own words:

There are fewer job opportunities for recent college graduates that have stable pay and benefits. This begins to be a factor in thinking about work. Often, there are large student loans with low-paying jobs being offered to pay them off. People seem to switch career paths multiple times now. That's very different.

They're getting married later, having children later. Less responsibility means less pressure and obligation to settle into a good job with benefits. People are renting versus buying, traveling, dating, trying their own self-employment ideas. The struggle with contentment and the whole push to find yourself make settling into a job more difficult.

There's less pressure to be a breadwinner because women are working. There's a push to find work that is meaningful more so than to find a job that pays well. Ambition looks different.

For many, it's not working. *Very rarely* have I had a girlfriend share that she was struggling because her husband worked too much or was too fixated on making money and being successful. One mutual friend who's a male said, "I struggle with finding the balance between working too much, but I try to remember what matters most. My wife has never said to me, 'I wish you put more hours in,' or, 'I wish you were not home with me and the kids as much.'"

A mid-thirties man in our office added that many of his peers are spending excessive amounts of "guy" time on sports, video games, outdoor recreation, etc. These are wholesome, fun things to do, but not when we do them at the expense of family and work.

We all want and need downtime and guy time, but our families need us too—they need us to lead, protect, and provide for them.

If this hits too close to home for you, consider this advice about work from the apostle Paul:

> In the name of the Lord Jesus Christ, we command you, brothers and sisters, to keep away from every believer who is idle and disruptive and does not live according to the teaching you received from us. For you yourselves know how *you ought to follow our example. We were not idle* when we were with you, nor did we eat anyone's food without paying for it. On the contrary, we worked night and day, *laboring and toiling so that we would not be a burden to any of you.* We did this, not because we do not have the right to such help, but in order to offer ourselves as *a model for you to imitate.* For even when we were with you, we gave you this rule: "The one who is unwilling to work shall not eat."
>
> We hear that some among you are idle and disruptive. They are not busy; they are busybodies. Such people we command and urge in the Lord Jesus Christ to *settle down and earn the food they eat.*
>
> *2 Thessalonians 3:6–12, emphasis added*

Work is a place to make plans and build for the future, but in prayerful submission to God's will.

Pounding in the breast of every man is an intense desire to lead a more significant life—to find the cause we talked about in chapter 1. A man's most innate need is his need to be significant—to find meaning and purpose in life, to make a difference, to accomplish something with his life. It makes sense, then, that men have ambitions.

How we each pursue this significance is what really differentiates one man from the next. We can pursue significance in both appropriate and inappropriate ways. The difference is not so much in what we do but why we do it—our motives.

> Now listen, you who say, "Today or tomorrow we will go to this or that city, spend a year there, carry on business and make money." Why, you do not even know what will happen tomorrow. What is your life? You are a mist that appears for a little while and then vanishes. Instead, you ought to say, "If it is the Lord's will, we will live and do this or that."
> *James 4:13–15*

Notice the verse is not saying not to make plans. It's saying the opposite. It's saying to make plans, but in submission to God's will. Submission is what can protect you from overambition.

Do you think you have been pursuing significance in a right way? Ultimately, to achieve a success that really matters, we each must balance our desire for vocational success against our other priorities, namely, God, our wives, and our children.

Caution: As men we tend to compartmentalize our families while we're at work but not our work while we're with our families. Our bodies are at home, but our minds are still at work. Striking a right balance between work and family is a cornerstone of achieving a true happiness.

HOW TO FIND A SATISFYING JOB

What if you or someone you care about can't enthusiastically say, "This is what I'm supposed to be doing, right here, right now—even if it's hard"? If you can't, then consider getting a new job!

Here's a letter I wrote to Robert with a lot of hard-earned lessons that can help you or a friend find that satisfying job.

And even if you're not "in the market" for a new job, this section will definitely give you practical ideas to help you think about your vocational calling, "win the respect of outsiders," and "find satisfaction in . . . toilsome labor under the sun."

Dear Robert,

Thanks for sharing your struggle to find a new career. Finding a new position that really satisfies isn't easy. The search can create many anxious moments.

I'm praying that God will bless you with an occupation you can love—one that will make you feel most happy, most alive, and most useful.

Of course, there's an urgency. There are bills to pay, a wife to keep happy, and kids to feed. What I would like to do, though, is ask you to set aside the urgency for a moment. Here are a few big-picture thoughts to consider.

Balance

I've watched you over the years, Robert. Whoever gets you gets a good man. You're a hard worker. They will be blessed. What I want to encourage you to consider, however, is a job that allows you to lead a more balanced life.

You've always zoomed around at the speed of light. You told me, though, that you wanted more time to spend with the Lord, your wife, and your children. What I'm suggesting is to find a position that will allow you to, for example, have time to meditate on sentences in the Bible rather than racing off to an early appointment. Or enable you to knock off early to watch your son's game.

When someone asks me the question, "How are you doing?" I hope to be able to say, "Busy and balanced." To be busy is good. To be busy and balanced is better. Just a thought, but as your friend, I think you could use a little more balance. Why not use this as an opportunity to make it happen?

You mentioned on the phone that it has been hard for you to discern what God may be saying to you. If I remember correctly, you said, "I don't want to miss God's will. I don't trust myself." But how do you do that? Here are a few suggestions.

A Sense of Mission and Calling

Remember that every vocation is holy to the Lord. Look for a job that gives you a sense of mission—a sense that you are part of something that will leave the world a better place. If it's driving a delivery truck, then know you are part of an international system of moving products to improve the quality of life for millions of people. Your company enables families to have dignity, earn a respectable income, provide for health care benefits, and meet social needs.

To make your work more than "just a job" means to bring the right attitude to your work. Don't go looking for a mere job, but a position that helps you fulfill God's calling on your life.

How You Are Wired

Here are three sets of words that can help you zero in on what types of occupations will motivate and stimulate you. For each of the three sets, circle the one word with which you most identify. Make a snap decision here. Don't analyze it. Go with your first impulse.

1. Visionary   Planner   Executer
2. Innovator   Adapter   Adopter
3. Designer   Developer   Maintainer*

*Adapted from Bobb Biehl's terms

As you can see, these are great clues about the types of work you may be drawn toward. For example, if you are an executer, you would go crazy if someone told you to draw up the plan. If you are a maintainer, you may enjoy property management but probably not architecture. If you are an innovator, you would feel stifled in a job that allowed no creativity.

How are you wired? What does that tell you about yourself, and about the types of positions that would satisfy you long-term?

Practical Considerations

Here are some practical questions to help you select the right position:

1. What are your social needs? We each have an appetite for a certain level of social interaction. You may love people but find too much social interaction tiring. In that case, you would want a position that gives you some space. Not, for example, customer service.

2. What are your health/stress needs? Some people thrive in high-pressure jobs. Most don't. If in your first look at a job you see clues that it involves a lot of stress, guess what? It will be more stressful a month later. Look for a twenty-first-century employer who doesn't want to "own" you. Look for one who will honor you as a human being and help you lead a balanced life.

3. What is your long-term vocational goal? You may find that you are not qualified to do what you really want to do. In that case, you may need additional training/education. If so, don't take a position that won't let you get it. If you have a goal that requires capital or heavy experience—say, owning a business or teaching

at a college—then you may have to take it in stages. Apply long-term thinking in a short-term world.

Wild Card

There is one question that deserves a look. Assuming time and money were no object, what would you do if you could do anything you wanted? Now ask yourself, Is it really such a wild idea? What adjustments would you have to make? Would they be worth it? What does your wife think? Will there ever be a better time? Probably not. Instead of asking, "Why?" ask, "Why not?"

Occupational Ministry

Whenever a godly man changes his work, it's not unusual for the thought to go through his mind, *I wonder if I should go into ministry*. The technical answer is that every job is ministry. Your ministry is to build the kingdom and tend the culture. That includes not only spiritual enterprises, but "in the world" vocations. Some may be called, but for most it is a wistful, fleeting thought. Unless you can't be happy unless you are in ministry, it's probably an interesting idea but not a calling.

Conclusion

Robert, I hope this has been helpful. Here are the questions I've raised in this letter. Why not spend a few minutes thinking them through? [And reader, why don't you do the same for this chapter's call to action?]

- How are you wired?
- What does that tell you about yourself, and about the types of positions that would satisfy you in the long term?

- What are your social needs?
- What are your health/stress needs?
- What is your long-term vocational goal?
- Assuming time and money were no object, what would you do if you could do anything you wanted? Why would you not do it?

Your friend always,
Pat

CONCLUSION

There is no greater feeling than to believe, "This is what I'm supposed to be doing, right here, right now—even if it's hard." This idea, when fully understood and genuinely believed, can change everything.

I hope, like Christopher, you already know your work is worthwhile. But I also hope you have gained or renewed a biblical perspective—a theology of work—about just how important your work is in the bigger scheme of things. You will be most satisfied when you fully understand and genuinely believe these truths:

- You were created to do real work that makes a real difference.
- Work is a calling for which you are ordained by God.
- Every vocation has dignity.
- Every vocation is holy to the Lord.
- Work is hard because of the Fall.
- Work is not just a platform for ministry; it *is* ministry.
- Every interaction is an opportunity to bring glory and honor to Christ.

- There is always a higher purpose to the work you're doing.
- Doing your work well is a testimony in and of itself.
- It is good to enjoy your work and find it satisfying.
- We need to take work seriously.
- Work is a place to make plans and build for the future, but in prayerful submission to God's will.

Long after you have forgotten the specifics of what we've been teaching in this chapter, I pray you will be guided by the Christian values we've discussed. I hope you will see that the work you are doing *is* ministry—that it will make a difference in the history of the world.

Here's a prayer for you to end this chapter:

Heavenly Father, thank you for the gift of enjoyable work—even when it's hard, and especially since half of our waking hours are devoted to our jobs. Lord, a biblical understanding of work has been presented in this chapter—a theology of work. I pray you will seal this understanding in my mind. To the extent that I don't enjoy my work, help me to use the ideas in "How to Find a Satisfying Job" to find work that will make me feel happy, alive, and useful for the glory and to the praise of Jesus. Amen.

*   *   *

In the next chapter, we're going to delve into one of the most confusing issues on the planet. Lust. This chapter is going to blow you away. Why? Because we're not going to spiritualize lust—or merely say what's politically and religiously correct. We're going to shoot for the truth—biblical truth. But first, please answer the questions.

Reflection and Small Group Discussion Questions

1. The big idea for this chapter is, "There is no greater feeling than to believe, 'This is what I'm supposed to be doing, right here, right now—even if it's hard.'" Do you feel that way, and why or why not?

2. What has been your theology of work? What have you learned or been reminded of in this chapter about the biblical view of work that you think will have a big influence on you?

3. Assuming time and money were no object, what would you do if you could do anything you wanted?

EIGHT

LUST

The Right Way to Deal with This Powerful Drive

"You have heard that it was said, 'You shall not commit adultery.' But I tell you that anyone who looks at a woman lustfully has already committed adultery with her in his heart."

MATTHEW 5:27–28

The practical solution to lust (and other sexual immorality) for most men is to get married and enjoy regular sex with their wife.

At a conference away from home, several pastors went to lunch together and were waited on by a strikingly beautiful, sensuous waitress. You could hear the sexual energy crackle in the air.

The temptation they felt to lust was so arresting that each man muttered his order into his menu so as not to stare. As she exited into the kitchen to place their orders, they all sat speechless staring at their place mats.

As Mark Rutland told the story to our Bible study group, the senior man finally broke the ice in his own inimitable way. "Well, God hath made the heavens and the earth."

They all nodded in agreement. "Oh, yes."

Then he said, "And all that is in them hath God made."

"Yes, that's right," they agreed.

"And also all humanity hath God made," he continued.

"Yes, God made humanity," they chimed in perfect cadence.

Then the older pastor nodded his head toward the kitchen door where their waitress had just disappeared and said, "And God hath made some nifty humanity, hath he not?"

They all howled, and the spell was broken. Nobody said a word, but as they looked around the table, they could see it in each other's eyes. *I felt it when she walked up to the table, did you feel it? Yeah, I felt it. I forgive you. Do you forgive me? Yes, I forgive you. Are you all right? Yeah, I'm all right.* And it was over. But it happened. It happened because that's what happens to men.

If even pastors can be so easily tempted to lust, one thing should be crystal clear: no man is immune from the temptation to lust. As one man put it, "My three greatest temptations are money, pride, and bikinis." Any man who says he doesn't struggle with the temptation to lust is lying. Plain and simple.

THE PROBLEM

Sexual attraction is one of the most powerful, primal forces God has created. Every man feels it, undeniably. When used the way God intends, sex is beautiful, even holy.

It's not exactly news, but we live in a culture that glorifies lust and sexual immortality. It's ubiquitous. In our sex-saturated culture, it's almost impossible to watch or read an interesting story that doesn't have at least soft porn (erotic or suggestive images intended to arouse), such as simulating intercourse under the covers.

Also not news, our sexual desire is one of the most easily corrupted and difficult to tame of all human desires. So in this chapter we're going to clarify what the Bible says about sex and lust by discussing some things that may be new for you or, at the minimum, clear up some confusion.

We'll answer questions like, What's the difference between "looking" and "lusting?" What's wrong with looking? When does looking become lusting? What is lust? Why is lust a sin? What is the difference between the temptation to lust and lust?

Talking about lust is not comfortable. Not in public, and certainly not in mixed company, so churches don't typically teach on lust.

Personally, I cannot recall ever hearing a teaching or sermon on lust beyond "Don't do it." I get it. It's awkward. In fact, I have always felt too uncomfortable to teach this material in depth at the Man in the Mirror Bible Study until, essentially, I was forced to as part of my preparation for writing this chapter!

That's why throughout this chapter we're going to dig deep for the biblical and practical ideas that will make us feel more prepared and confident to deal with lust the right way.

If we're going to solve the problems created by the corruption of sex, however, we first need to understand what uncorrupted sex looks like.

GOD'S DESIGN FOR SEX

Sex is God's gift to a married man and woman so they can have children and enjoy physical intimacy with each other. However, if you have chosen to remain single, whether for now or forever, I think you will also be encouraged by the ideas in this chapter.

The passage that addresses sex most comprehensively is 1 Corinthians 7:1–9. There Paul set the boundaries for holy sex in response to questions posed in a letter from the Christians in Corinth. Paul wrote back about sex outside of marriage: "Now for the matters you wrote about: 'It is good for a man not to have sexual relations with a woman.' *But since sexual immorality is occurring . . .*" (1 Corinthians 7:1–2, emphasis added).

The first thing we see is that sexual immorality is nothing new. As then, so now. Testosterone levels haven't suddenly spiked. Sex sins have been occurring in every generation. Paul continued: ". . . each man should have sexual relations with his own wife, and each woman with her own husband."

Marriage is God's design for sex. Notice the words *wife* and *husband*. But wait, there's more! Paul went on to say that married people should have sex regularly:

The husband should fulfill his marital duty to his wife, and likewise the wife to her husband. The wife does not have authority over her own body but yields it to her husband. In the same way, the husband does not have authority over his own body but yields it to his wife.

1 Corinthians 7:3–4

Which brings us to the big idea for this chapter: the practical solution to lust (and other sexual immorality) for most men is to get married and enjoy regular sex with their wife.

Paul amplified this in even more detail: *"Do not deprive each other except perhaps by mutual consent and for a time, so that you may devote yourselves to prayer. Then come together again so that Satan will not tempt you because of your lack of self-control"* (1 Corinthians 7:5, emphasis added).

I don't know how it could be any clearer: If you have chosen marriage, Satan will tempt you if you don't have regular sex. If you want to go on a "sex fast," you can, but only by mutual agreement and not for long. To be blunt, if you're not horny, you're more likely to exercise self-control.

Bottom line: Our sexual design is a powerful, primal force. Having regular intimate relations with our wives is the biblical solution to block the corruption of that design by sexual immorality, including lust.

Paul also has sex advice for single men. Unusual is the man who, like Paul, is called to celibacy. Paul commends it but quickly clarifies that it's better to get married than "burn with passion [lust]":

I say this as a concession, not as a command. I wish that all of you were as I am. But each of you has your own gift from God; one has this gift, another has that. Now to the unmarried and the widows I say: It is good for them to stay unmarried, as I do. *But if they cannot control themselves,*

they should marry, for it is better to marry than to burn with
passion.

                           1 Corinthians 7:6–9, emphasis added

After his wife spitefully divorced him, Kevin went off the
rails with alcohol, barhopping, and promiscuity. He ended up
living with a woman. He said, "I know this isn't right. But I just
can't control my passions. I'm burning up with lust. I need to get
married." Even though he was living in sin, he still recognized it
and eventually did the right thing:

> *If anyone is worried that he might not be acting honorably*
> toward the virgin he is engaged to, and if his passions are
> too strong and he feels he ought to marry, he should do as
> he wants. He is not sinning. *They should get married.*
>
>   *1 Corinthians 7:36, emphasis added*

Getting married and having regular sex is how God designed
for you to channel your sexual desire. We need to know that!
However, this is not a chapter on how to have great sex, but on
how to deal with lustful thoughts.

Every man is wired by God to appreciate beauty of all kinds—
sunrises, mountain vistas, newborns, soccer, and so on. But a
woman falls into an altogether different and exclusive category.
As G. K. Chesterton said, "Keeping to one woman is a small price
for so much as seeing one woman."[1]

Having thoughts about sex is normal. It's biology. Research is
vague and unreliable, but one study found that men think about
sex nineteen times a day on average.[2]

God does not put any limits on sex; he does put limits
on sexual immorality. Let's distinguish between what lust is
and isn't.

WHAT *ISN'T* LUST?

In the story of David and Bathsheba, it's clear God wanted to preserve a story that answers many of the questions men have about lust.

As men, the main way we experience sexual attraction and arousal is through sight. One night, King David couldn't sleep. He was walking around on the roof terrace of his palace when he saw a woman—a very beautiful woman—bathing on the roof of another man's home. So far, not a problem. He didn't go up to his roof to look for a naked woman so he could be sexually aroused (provided that's true, and I think we can plausibly assume it's true). This is a huge point: *seeing isn't seeking, looking isn't lusting.*

Next, he sensed attraction. That's still normal. Whether it's being surprised by a sensuous waitress, the suggestively dressed coed who attracts your attention at the gym, a sex scene you didn't seek out, or any other visual cue, it's not a sin. Attraction is essential to procreation and the perpetuation of our species.

Sex, of course, is everywhere. But in our cultural moment, seduction is inescapable. We're bombarded. The visage of a shapely woman walking down the street comes to mind, or a scantily clad model who suddenly appears while scrolling through what should be a harmless news feed. But these images burst into our minds like a guest who doesn't knock.

When a sex scene comes on your screen, is that for you a temptation to lust or the sin of lust? It depends. It's not lust to "stumble" onto a temptation. Having a thought pop into your mind about having intercourse with a woman is not itself immoral. It's a fine line: thoughts are temptations, not sins.

You can't keep someone from knocking on your door, but you can decide whom you invite to come inside.

Still, you have to take personal responsibility to control attraction. It's what you do next that counts, as illustrated in Mike's story.

MIKE'S WANDERING EYES:
SAVED BY THREE PEAS

Mike loves God with all his heart. Yet he made a regular practice of checking out beautiful women. One day, he realized that what he was doing was a sin against his wife. He made a commitment to stop looking and lusting.

"One day not much later," Mike said, "I was sitting in a restaurant just finishing my meal. Out of the corner of my eye, I noticed a very sensual woman walk into the restaurant. I was determined that I was not going to look at her and lust.

"I didn't know what to do, so I prayed and asked God for help. As it happened, there were about three peas left on my plate. I decided to focus on those peas and began to stare real hard.

"I felt like my head was caught in a giant tug-of-war. One force pulled my jaw upward to look at this woman. The other force yanked my eyes back toward those three peas. It was a bare-knuckles brawl between old habit and new commitment. My face was half twisted toward her, but my eyes bulged out to stay glued on those peas.

"Finally the battle began to subside. A few moments later it was over. I had won. God gave a spiritual victory. I still am tempted to lust, but God has given me the power to have victory every time I ask him to help."

A couple weeks later, Mike's wife, Sarah, asked him, "Are you intentionally not looking at other women?"

When Mike said, "Yes," Sarah said, "You have no idea how secure it makes me feel to know that you only have eyes for me."

Wandering eyes is, of course, nothing new. Even Job, the friend of God, had to deal with that kind of sexual temptation. Look at what he said: "I made a covenant with my eyes not to look lustfully at a young woman" (Job 31:1).

Amazing! That's the same covenant Mike made! There's no

reason you can't make it your covenant too. I did many years ago. I haven't been able to keep it fully, but I've sure done a lot better having made the commitment than not.

Job's covenant requires will power—your will and God's power. We can't do anything long-term unless we acknowledge that we are spiritual "invalids" who need the Holy Spirit to strengthen us. Let's be honest: you can't resist googling something you shouldn't or thumbing through the *Victoria's Secret* catalog on your own—at least not every time. If you haven't already done so, consider making "Job's covenant" right now as a call to action. That's what Mike did.

GOD'S DESIGN DOES NOT INCLUDE BATHSHEBA

Unlike Mike, David did not turn away. Unlike Job, he did not make a covenant with his eyes. Instead, he allowed himself to burn with passion for Bathsheba. He graduated from "seeing" her to "watching" her. Instead of turning away, he stared. Still temptation, but at this point it was either turn away or lust was inevitable. Letting your thoughts linger is what puts "attraction" on track to become "lust."

You probably know the rest of the story. He sent for her and had sex with her. She became pregnant. He plotted the death of her husband, which also resulted in the deaths of at least two other men. Then he took Bathsheba for his own wife.

Lust is sexual desire out of control.

Even though David was a man after God's own heart, God was grieved. Although God forgave him (he forgives all who seek forgiveness), the consequences described by the prophet Nathan are breathtaking: David's baby died; his son Absalom led a revolt; David had to flee into exile; and Absalom had sex with David's concubines in public view.

Beyond the potential for all kinds of disease and public humiliation, adultery, while forgivable, sometimes does permanent and irreparable damage to our relationships and the people we love.

LUST IS "MENTAL" ADULTERY

Because of the Ten Commandments, everyone knows that adultery is a sin: "You shall not commit adultery" (Deuteronomy 5:18).

There are two kinds of adultery. Adultery type 1 occurs when a married man *physically* has sex with a woman not his wife or when an unmarried man sleeps with a married woman. (And fornication is when an unmarried man has sex with an unmarried woman).

Most of the physical adultery I've seen through our work with men is the result of inappropriate work relationships with coworkers. One or both feel emotionally neglected, and they get attached. And then one thing leads to another.

But there's a second kind of adultery, as explained by Jesus in the Sermon on the Mount: "You have heard that it was said, 'You shall not commit adultery.' But I tell you that *anyone who looks at a woman lustfully has already committed adultery with her in his heart*" (Matthew 5:27–28, emphasis added). Adultery type 2 is *mentally* having sex with someone not your wife, or lust.

Lust is "mental" adultery. Jesus says you don't have to commit the "physical" act to commit adultery. "Mental" adultery is also adultery. So, yes, lust is sinful. It's a departure from God's plan for sex. And while women can lust too, notice that Jesus pegs lust as a particularly masculine issue.

Nevertheless, "mental" adultery is not the same as "physical" adultery. Lust is "thinking" about or "imagining" sex with a woman not your wife. Here's a good working definition for lust:

*Lust is mental adultery by seeking out ways to look at, watch,
listen to, read about, or covet any woman other than your wife
to arouse yourself sexually, escalated if you masturbate.*

Lust is more than accidentally stumbling across sexually
explicit material or having a sex dream. It's you proactively seeking
sexual stimulation.

If you "seek out" movies for their sex scenes so you can be
aroused, that's the sin of lust. When a sex scene shows up unex-
pectedly, if you hit rewind, that's lust.

If you're watching a video, television program, or movie
and a man and woman simulate the act of sex, it's pornography.
Whether you call it porn or soft porn—Supreme Court Justice
Potter Stewart said in a 1964 case, "I know it when I see it"[3]—we
know in our hearts we shouldn't be watching.

And in case you're wondering, wanting to have sex with your
wife is not lust. Why? Because Jesus says lust is adultery, and you
can't commit adultery with your own wife.

And now since I brought it up, I guess we need to address
masturbation.

IS IT WRONG TO MASTURBATE?

I first wrote about masturbation to teenage boys in *The Young Man
in the Mirror*. I'll tell you essentially what I told them.

First and foremost, the Bible does not specifically address
masturbation. Which is interesting, because it easily could
have. So, what I'm about to tell you is opinion—please read it
accordingly.

You can masturbate and not sin. When puberty begins at age
thirteen or so, a man's body begins to produce testosterone, which

is the male hormone. Testosterone produces a sexual drive in a man. Testosterone makes men horny.

It is normal to want to masturbate. Men are going to masturbate for pleasure. That's all there is to it. I wouldn't worry too much about it with two cautions.

- First, don't fantasize about women and intercourse. Don't look at pictures of women or watch videos. Why? Because that is lust.
- Second, don't allow yourself to habitually masturbate. It's almost impossible to define what's habitual, but you probably already know if "habitual" describes you.

Is there anybody who doesn't feel uncomfortable and awkward right now? I certainly do!

Again, the Bible is silent on this subject, so you will need to draw your own conclusion.

WHAT CAN YOU DO WHEN YOU'RE ATTRACTED?

When you see a beautiful woman and feel an attraction, here's what you should do: Pause and say, "Thank you, God, for this beautiful woman whom you have reverently and wonderfully made. I pray she knows you, or one day will know you, the way I know you." And then move on.

But don't walk around the block for another look. Temptation is seeing a pretty woman. Sin is walking around the block for another look.

XXXchurch.com, a ministry dedicated to fighting our culture's pornography problem, has a clever way of drawing the line between appreciation of the opposite sex and lust: "Look once, you're human; look twice, you're a man; look three times, you just disrespected your wife."[4]

We need to take personal responsibility. The apostle Paul wrote forcefully, "Flee from sexual immorality. All other sins a person commits are outside the body, but whoever sins sexually, sins against their own body" (1 Corinthians 6:18).

Once I was taking a walk before dawn. As I passed by one home, I noticed the light was on behind the translucent glass of a large bathroom window.

No creature was stirring, and pitch-black engulfed the rest of the street, so I was doubly startled to see the outline of a woman who seemed to be dancing or doing exercises behind the window.

I've been a Christian for a long time. I had just finished a beautiful time with the Lord in prayer. Yet in the blink of an eye, some force lunged toward me and tried to drag me toward the window for a closer look. I got out of there as fast as I could, but it frightens me that it could happen at all!

"Fleeing" obviously requires some self-control. You'll never be able to consistently flee in your own strength. You will need to believe in your heart that fleeing is one of the ways Jesus wants you to demonstrate your love and devotion to him as part of a grateful response for his mercy, grace, and love. To flee requires the kind of "self-control" that is a fruit of the Holy Spirit (Galatians 5:22–23).

However, let's keep it real. Nobody is forcing us to lust. Lust is our own fault. Here are several practical examples of how you can flee sexual temptation:

- If you surf YouTube for comedy skits and movie previews but inevitably end up watching videos you know you shouldn't be watching, then don't surf YouTube alone.

- If every time you check your team's score on the *Sports Illustrated* website you also gawk at the bathing suit ads, then check the scores somewhere else.
- If being on your phone when you're home alone leads you to search for the wrong things, then don't get on your phone when you're home alone.
- Don't have a regular female lunch buddy or a female workout partner at the gym.
- Don't travel with a woman.
- When a sex scene starts on a TV show, fast-forward through that section.

If you are where you shouldn't be, you're more likely to do what you shouldn't do. So know what your triggers are, and then just don't pull them. Why intentionally flirt with disaster? Flee!

And if you do believe fleeing is the right thing to do but still struggle—or in the words of Jesus, you find "the spirit is willing, but the flesh is weak" (Matthew 26:41)—then you can give a brother or your small group permission to hold you accountable by regularly asking you how you're doing.

Maybe a group like the one that helped Joseph can help you too.

JOSEPH'S STORY: CARRY EACH OTHER'S BURDENS

In an earlier life, Joseph was one of the boys. He was never evil, but like many young men, Joseph was prone to talk about women and stare at the wrong kinds of pictures. Joseph married, and soon after he yielded his life to a personal faith in God. After his first child was born, he began to seriously settle down.

At his small group Bible study one morning, the group discussed sexual temptation. After the meeting, Joseph, a Christian for less than two years, pulled the leader aside.

"I need to talk about this," he said. "Frankly, I'm somewhat relieved. I thought I was the only Christian man alive who struggles with lust at the level I do. I've got it bad. Some days the temptation is such a spiritual battle all day long that I am completely exhausted by the time I get home. I feel like I've got two dogs inside me fighting."

If you have a less extreme struggle with lust, then being part of a small group and being open with them about your burdens will be helpful. Part of the mandate for a small group is to "carry each other's burdens" (Galatians 6:2).

But heed these two cautions:

- Even if you have a group of men asking you weekly, "Have you sought out any sexually explicit materials this week?" you can still lie to them.
- Run as fast as you can from any group that reinforces the notion that all men "struggle" with lust and so it's acceptable. Men in those groups can rarely testify to God's power to change their lives in this area.

Let's say you tried all of the above but still struggle. What can you do if lust has been a losing battle for you?

STEVE'S STORY: WHAT CAN YOU DO IF YOU STILL STRUGGLE WITH PORN?

Consider Steve. His struggle with pornography started at the age of eleven. He was born again in his late twenties but continued to live a secret life of lust. Steve's wife said, "I always felt like there was a third person in our bedroom. I never felt cherished. So I just went ahead and did my duty."

Even when he turned fifty, Steve was still struggling with unwanted sexual behavior. He said, "PG-13 gives me hungry eyes."

Finally he faced the fact that he had a problem he could not solve on his own. He just got so tired of trying to conceal and manage his secret life. He said, "I had a broken mind."

Steve's message for you is that healing can come quickly. "I tried to stop, but nothing worked until the leader of a ministry that specializes in sexual purity said, 'One hundred percent disclosure in brokenness, humility, continued transparency, and confession to the people you care about is the only way out.'" So Steve did just that. He confessed everything to his wife, children, pastor, friends—everyone.

When Steve finally confessed he had been living a fake life, at first his wife just turned comatose. Finally she threw a book across the table. They have had to work through this in stages, but the good news is that within the first one hundred days, the hard work was behind him.

Steve has now been free from bondage to pornography for three years. "I'm still tempted all the time," he said. "But now I immediately text my wife and tell her what's happening." For her part, Steve's wife said, "How can I help him if I don't know everything that's going on?"

MIGUEL'S BATTLE AND VICTORY OVER UNWANTED SEXUAL BEHAVIOR

When Miguel was seven years old, he stumbled across one of his dad's magazines. The pictures of naked women made his head spin. About the same time, he became aware of lusty late-night shows. He started getting up to watch them after his parents went to bed. The tentacles of porn started to wrap around his young brain, which commenced a fifteen-year battle with unwanted sexual behavior.

Once during a middle school sleepover, his friends introduced him to pornographic websites that he didn't even know existed. By the time Miguel was in the eighth grade, he was in a free-fall struggle with porn, eventually escalating to more hardcore genres. Objectifying women and thinking about sex constantly became a daily struggle. After school he headed straight home while his parents were still at work and "medicated" himself three or four times a day.

As a teen, Miguel was riddled by shame and guilt, convinced he was the only one with his problem. When he fell for a girl at the age of thirteen, his bondage to unwanted sexual behavior was poisoning their relationship until, finally, he confessed everything to her. She forgave him, and, eventually they became engaged.

Using "willpower," Miguel was gradually weaning himself off pornography, but his fiancée caught him relapsing several times. Thinking she was not good enough, she became self-conscious and developed an eating disorder, eventually dropping down to ninety-five pounds. Although his family had never regularly attended church, when a friend invited him to attend, he accepted. That day, an ashamed Miguel came forward to pray and seek God's help during a church service.

Even though he became a follower of Jesus, Miguel still wanted the best the world had to offer. "I became a poser. I had a great job, but I was constantly struggling in the dark with my lust. My relationship with Christ was one-sided. I had one foot in the world and one foot in the church. I wanted to get close enough to Jesus to reap all of the benefits of salvation but not have to sacrifice anything on my end—including porn, despite wanting to be free from it.

"Everything came to a stop when I took a friend request from a woman I didn't know who asked me to Skype with her. She recorded our session and then tried to blackmail me for money. When I refused, she set up a fake Facebook page with my name and picture, uploaded the video of me, and sent a friend request to all my Facebook friends. What I thought would be a quick moment of indulgence turned into a traumatizing, life-altering moment within a matter of minutes.

"My world began to fall apart. I was freaking out. I was that guy who was overly concerned about my self-image. And now my darkest secret had been exposed on the world's biggest social media platform. My phone wouldn't stop—calls, texts, emails. Facebook quickly shut down the fake site, but the damage was done. That was the end of my relationship with my fiancée. I can't blame her—I put her through hell. Everything that happened to me was my own fault.

"That night, unable to sleep, I cried out to God but heard nothing. I felt abandoned and hopeless. In desperation, I pulled out my Bible app, spun the screen, and decided to read the first Scripture my finger landed on. As if on cue, the Lord landed me at Proverbs 7, an entire chapter describing how men need to beware of an adulterous woman.

"I went to church that Sunday and was halfway to the altar before the pastor had finished inviting people who wanted to confess their sins and give their lives to Jesus to come forward."

Today, Miguel is living in victory over pornography. He said, "That doesn't mean I'm not tempted. I still have pornographic images pop into my mind, and I'm not perfect."

I asked Miguel, "What would you tell men who struggle with pornography?"

"First, tell them they can be free from compulsive behavior, but it's going to be a lifelong battle. They're going to be tempted every day. They need to take action when they are in a position of strength, not after they've already started playing with fire. It's much harder to turn back at that point. So they need to be intentional."

Then I asked Miguel, who now lectures on porn and sexual purity, "How did you get free? What are the intentional steps you took?"

Miguel explained his own intentional plan, which I've summarized for you below (this is the actual plan he still does). If you have a problem with unwanted sexual behavior—whether you most resemble Kevin, Mike, Joseph, Steve, or Miguel—I've included a blank line after each idea so you can make your own intentional plan as a call to action.

Miguel's Intentional Plan

Identity: Find your identity in Christ—understand what that means and what a relationship with Jesus means you have access to.

Confession: Confess to everyone you can—all of it, get it in the light, get it in the open. First to a trusted handful of individuals, including your wife if married, church leaders, and eventually others over time—make it a lifestyle. It's tough but essential for healing. A weight will lift off your shoulders. Walking in the light should become a lifestyle. Begin living in such a way that there will not be anything to confess because everything will already be in the light (more on this below).

A Group: Focus on building a grace-based relationship with Jesus. Do this with a group of other like-minded men. Plugging into an accountability group connected to a reputable sexual purity program is highly beneficial.

Accountability: Tell three to five guys, "I don't want to keep secrets anymore," and ask them to hold you accountable by calling or texting to check on how you're doing. Ask them to monitor your computer with software like Covenant Eyes. Include as appropriate your wife, friends, parents, men from church.

Purge: Purge all pornographic content from your home, your devices, your social media accounts, etc. Delete apps, people, websites, etc. that may be triggering lust. Stop visiting locations or hanging out with people who are not a good influence on you. It's not worth it.

Counsel: Find a good Christian counselor.

Health: Take care of yourself through diet, exercise, sleep.

Retreat: Go on a men's retreat with your church, especially one that has a session on sexual purity.

Mentor: Find an older man who also once struggled with pornography and is now walking in victory.

Serve: Focus on helping others, which takes healing to the next level. Living a life for self will eventually leave you empty and lead you back into your bondage. We are called to not just sit on our freedom but to use it to help others get free as well. "Therefore, go . . ."

Temptation: The best way to overcome temptation is to not put yourself in a position where you will be tempted. But when it does come, change your circumstances. Leave, pray for "a way of escape," play worship music, call a friend, consider the consequences, consider how Jesus or your spouse would feel/react, and remember you are never *really* alone when you are acting out. God is right there with you.

Sin: When you fail—and you will—confess to Jesus, receive his full pardon, accept his grace, and tell a confidential accountability friend.

ED COLE'S "CALL TO ACTION"

In this final section, I want us to discuss some family business—a challenge to confront our unwanted sexual behavior. If you are still trying to decide whether to follow Christ, we're not trying to tell you how you should live. As the apostle Paul said, "I wrote to you in my letter not to associate with sexually immoral people—not at all meaning the people of this world who are immoral, or the greedy and swindlers, or idolaters. In that case you would have to leave this world" (1 Corinthians 5:9–10).

However, if you are a professing Christian, I hope you will take this very seriously.

Ed Cole, a pioneer in men's ministry, wrote a story in his magnum opus, *Maximized Manhood*, about a men's retreat in Eugene, Oregon. During a long flight to get to the event, the Lord gave him a very powerful message for the men. When he arrived at the podium, as was his custom, he had the men stand for prayer. Before they sat down, he looked them in the eye and called them to action:

> If you are here tonight and committing adultery, fornication, homosexuality, incest, or habitual masturbation; indulging in pornography; gratifying yourself in sexual fantasies or any other kind of sex sin, I command you in the name of Jesus Christ of Nazareth to repent, and be restored to a right relationship with God the Father by being reconciled through Jesus Christ and the power of the Holy Spirit.[5]

And this was at the very start of the retreat! A confused hush fell over the room as men tried to grasp what they had just heard.

And then, suddenly, the room erupted. Men's hands shot in the air! Some of the men were in business, some in common labor; some were young, some old. In unison they began to cry out to God in praise and worship. Those men had been aching for someone to tell them truth, and that night someone did.

That night, the Holy Spirit peeled back the roof of a small mountain chapel and flooded the room with the grace to forgive, heal, and restore those men where they most keenly felt the sting of the lack of the gospel's impact in their lives.

Are you struggling with sexual sins? Is so, let me say to you, as Ed Cole said to those men, "In the name of Jesus, repent and be restored to a right relationship with God the Father by being reconciled through Jesus Christ and the power of the Holy Spirit." Here's a prayer for you to pray in response to this challenge.

A "CALL TO ACTION" PRAYER

Lord Jesus, thank you so much for your Word, that we have not been left alone to sort all this out. You've given us ample advice, wisdom, counsel, direction, and even commands on how to walk out our sexual lives in this world, and so we thank you for that. By faith, I repent of all my sex sins— indulging in pornography, sexual fantasies, habitual masturbation, heterosexual or homosexual immorality, incest, adultery, and every other kind of sexual sin. By faith, I ask you to restore me to a right relationship with God the Father through the power of your Holy Spirit. Please tutor the truth of your Word to our hearts so that we might be able to have victory in our temptations and battles with lust. We ask this in Jesus' name. Amen.

The beauty of Christ's gospel is that no matter what you've done, you can be forgiven. Forgiveness is there for the asking: "If we confess our sins, he is faithful and just and will forgive us our sins and purify us from all unrighteousness" (1 John 1:9).

In the future when you lust—and you will—pause and think about what you've done, and when you are genuinely sorry, simply thank Jesus that he already died for that sin, ask for his forgiveness, and move on.

Reflection and Small Group Discussion Questions

---

1. Do you agree that we live in a culture that glorifies lust and sexual immorality? How big of an issue is lust for you?

2. Does your view of how to channel your sexual desire match up with the Scriptures in this chapter? What have you read that's new to you, or that you're glad to be reminded of?

3. We should not pretend that "Jesus and me" and a lot of prayer, though important, are enough to conquer lust. We also need to take personal responsibility. Glance back through the chapter and decide what steps you will take to exercise self-control over sexual desire. Did you pray the "call to action" prayer? Do you understand how to confess your sins according to the promise in 1 John 1:9? If you are in a discussion group, have you heard any other ideas that might be helpful?

NINE

CULTURE

The Role of a Christian Man in Our Culture

Seek the peace and prosperity of the city to which
I have carried you into exile. Pray to the LORD for
it, because if it prospers, you too will prosper.

JEREMIAH 29:7

God wants each of us to go find some
unredeemed corner of culture and
claim it for the glory of Christ.

In the fable of "The Wise King," Kahlil Gibran tells about a powerful, wise, and much-loved king who lived in a distant land. In that land was a single well from which all the people had to draw their water.

One night a witch poisoned the well so that all who drank the water would become mad.

The next morning, all the people of the land, except the king and his ranking official, came as usual to drink from the well and did indeed go mad.

Throughout the rest of the day, the people whispered to each other, "Our king and his high official have gone mad and lost their reason. We cannot be ruled by a mad king. He must be dethroned!"

Word of this got back to the king and, not wanting to offend anyone, he sent his official to draw some water from the well, which they both then drank.

And the people rejoiced because their king had regained his reason.[1]

THE CURRENT CLIMATE

As in the fable, we increasingly live in a peculiar, upside-down culture where opinions are given the same credence as facts. Where the opinions of the masses sway the wisdom of leaders.

Enter social media. No one whispers anymore. We post. In a fraction of a second, with a simple click, civil people attack those they disagree with. Often without even knowing the other person. As marketing expert Mark Fisher observed in *Entrepreneur* magazine, "The deer have guns."[2]

One reason we are at each other's throats so much is that, because of social media and technology, we know so much more about each other's throats!

You know the issues: education, school violence, protecting innocent children, the economy, federal deficits, school debt, finding a job that pays well, racism, politics, human trafficking, the environment, poverty, social justice, fatherlessness, divorce, homelessness, gang violence, immigration, social media bullying, internet scams, sex scandals, police shootings, abortions, and disputes over how to define marriage and gender issues—to mention many of the more visible ones.

If the issues facing our culture could be solved with logic, they would have been resolved by now. There is poison in the water.

Trying to divine which way a culture like ours is going to go is like trying to guess which way a squirrel in the middle of the road is going to jump. One thing's for sure—cultures are constantly shifting. Our cultural moment is very different from the one we were in twenty years ago. And it's different from the one we'll be in twenty years from now.

I know you care about the issues ripping at our culture. No doubt you've wondered, *What can I do? I'm just one man.*

The twenty-four men I surveyed for this book overwhelmingly voted culture as one of their top issues. Their questions illustrate just how difficult it is for the Christian man to know how he should interact with today's culture: "On what basis do I accept cultural shifts? How can I stay true to my faith when so many around me are abandoning theirs? How do I deal with social media and digital addiction? How should Christians mix politics and faith, or should we? Why do we still have black churches, white churches, and Hispanic churches? How can I engage culture without coming off as critical? I want to be a Christian who makes a difference, but I don't want to be belligerent about it. How can I engage with such a rapidly vacillating culture?"

So how can we approach such a vast issue?

First, we'll explore how Jesus interacted with culture so we can establish the benchmark. Then we'll look at the stance of a Christian man toward culture in the current climate. Next, while we don't have space to cover every issue raised by the storyboard men, we'll look for inspiration from a couple of examples of cultural change. We'll end by helping you find or affirm your personal stance and calling to culture.

The big question for the Christian man about culture is, "Where in my community is my influence as a Christian needed most?" It could be any of the issues already mentioned or something else, such as addiction, teen pregnancy, or serving single moms.

Once identified—and this is the big idea for this chapter— *God wants each of us to go find some unredeemed corner of culture and claim it for the glory of Christ.* This idea goes to the heart of both the cultural mandate and the Great Commission. We are the stewards of Christ's gospel in a broken world.

The good news is that by activating the biblical principles in this chapter, men around the world are engaging and influencing culture for the glory of Jesus Christ, and you can too. You may already be in the game. If not, this is your invitation to suit up and take the field.

The best example of how to engage culture is Jesus Christ.

The Stance Jesus Took toward Culture

It's quite surprising that someone as opposed to the existing order as Jesus wouldn't try to replace it. But Jesus expressed no desire to *overthrow* or *replace* the existing culture. When Roman soldiers came to arrest him unjustly, he said to Peter (who had drawn a sword), "Put your sword back in its place . . . for all who draw the sword will die by the sword. Do you think I cannot call on my Father, and he will at once put at my disposal more than twelve legions of angels?" (Matthew 26:52–53)

Nor did he seek to *embrace* or *withdraw* from the culture. Instead, the stance of Jesus was to *engage* culture. He didn't come to install a new Christian culture. He came to "embed" the kingdom of God into the existing culture. How did he do that?

This year I'm reading through the four gospels once a month (eighty-nine chapters, so three chapters a day). While writing this chapter, I read the book of Matthew and saw something I'd never noticed before.

The *teachings* of Jesus are robust. Of course, he primarily focused on the kingdom of God. No surprise there. He also weighed in on virtually every issue confronting his current culture, including, for example, government, taxes, marriage, divorce, greed, and pride. That's part of his stance.

That said, all of the 34,450 recorded words of Jesus can be spoken in about ten thirty-minute sermons.[3] While Jesus obviously taught more than what is recorded, what we do have still only adds up to about five hours of teaching in a ministry that lasted for more than three years!

So what did Jesus do with his time? Most of his actual *time* was spent *serving* the real, practical needs of the people around him. Here's a good example from the passage leading up to the feeding of the four thousand:

> Great crowds came to him, bringing the lame, the blind, the crippled, the mute and many others, and laid them at his feet; and he healed them. The people were amazed when they saw the mute speaking, the crippled made well,

the lame walking and the blind seeing. And they praised
the God of Israel.

Jesus called his disciples to him and said, "I have compassion for these people; they have already been with me
three days and have nothing to eat. I do not want to send
them away hungry, or they may collapse on the way."

Matthew 15:30–32

This is the stance Jesus took: he met the practical needs of
people while explaining how the gospel applied to every aspect
of their eternal and temporal lives. So given his example, what
stance does Jesus want us to take?

Our Stance toward Culture

Perhaps you've heard the saying "in but not of" the world. It
comes from a prayer of Jesus, spoken just prior to his crucifixion,
often called his High Priestly Prayer. What makes it so remarkable
is that it's a prayer he specifically prayed for us!

"I will remain in the world no longer, but they are still *in
the world* . . . My prayer is not that you take them *out of the
world* but that you protect them from the evil one. They
are not *of the world,* even as I am not of it . . . As you sent
me into the world, *I have sent them into the world* . . . My
prayer is not for them alone. *I pray also for those who will
believe in me through their message.*"

John 17:11, 15–16, 18, 20, emphasis added

Jesus doesn't take us "out" of the world—which is quite
interesting because he could easily beam us up the moment we
believed. Obviously, God has what he considers a greater purpose
for us to remain "in" the world beyond our salvation. He "sent"

us "into" the world to engage the world, following the example of Jesus.

Jesus is coming back, but we don't know when, and it has already been two thousand years, so what do we do until he does? That would be an extraordinary dilemma if we were left to figure it out on our own!

Fortunately, we don't have to. Here's a powerful way you and I can engage culture, originally addressed to a badly broken Israelite culture:

> This is what the LORD Almighty, the God of Israel, says *to all those I carried into exile* from Jerusalem to Babylon: *"Build houses and settle down;* plant gardens and eat what they produce. *Marry and have sons and daughters;* find wives for your sons and give your daughters in marriage, so that they too may have sons and daughters. *Increase in number* there; do not decrease. Also, *seek the peace and prosperity of the city to which I have carried you into exile. Pray to the Lord for it, because if it prospers, you too will prosper."*
>
> *Jeremiah 29:4–7, emphasis added*

What's particularly interesting about being sent into the world is that "where" he sends us typically (though not always) means "right where you are." The apostle Paul wrote, "Brothers and sisters, each person, as responsible to God, should remain in the situation they were in when God called them" (1 Corinthians 7:24).

God knows where you are right now. He has you there for a reason. Look around. Where is the culture—*your* culture—under attack? Where is there a strong and obvious need for God's love and power? That's where you're needed, as this quote illustrates:

If I profess, with the loudest voice and the clearest exposition, every portion of the truth of God except precisely that little point which the world and the devil are at that moment attacking, I am not confessing Christ, however boldly I may be professing Christianity. Where the battle rages the loyalty of the soldier is proved; and to be steady on all the battlefield besides is mere flight and disgrace to him if he flinches at that one point.[4]

If you want to engage the culture, the questions are, "What are the practical needs around me that are going unmet? And once identified, what does loyalty to Jesus Christ look like?"

When I did the initial research for this book, racial reconciliation was a top concern among the men I surveyed. Let's look at an example that can help reclaim this corner of culture for the glory of Christ.

AN EXAMPLE OF RACIAL RECONCILIATION

As mentioned in the chapter on friendships, I became best friends with Tom Skinner. What I didn't mention is that Tom is an African American and I am a white man.

Tom helped me see that I could have lived my entire life and never known a black person personally, and it would not have affected the outcome of my life one iota. Tom helped me see that, as a result, I looked at racial injustice with apathy, or indifference.

But he also showed me that the average black man can't go three days without knowing how white people think because of employer/employee, landlord/tenant, and vendor/vendee relationships. Tom helped me see that, as a result, racial injustice left him feeling helpless and angry.

Tom and I became intentional friends. We made a commitment to get to know each other. What happened, basically, was that he took away a lot of my apathy and I took away a lot of his anger—just by hanging out together.

Tom often taught, "We are called to be the live demonstration of what's happening in the kingdom of God so that anytime someone wants to know what's going on in heaven, all they have to do is check with us."

Those were inspiring words. But it had never occurred to me that God might use those words to call my number and send me into the game.

When I was thirty-one years old, a racial disturbance erupted on Parramore Avenue in Orlando big enough to make national news because it included arson, vandalism, and looting. Our local sheriff, a neighbor of mine, was injured when a rock went through his windshield.

At the time we employed Merthie, a mature African American woman with whom we had become close, to help us clean our home once a week. She lived near Parramore Avenue. As partially recounted in my book *Pastoring Men*, the following day I went home for lunch and Merthie was there. It was awkward.

Finally I was able to blurt out, "Merthie, what do you think it's going to take for us to all figure out how to get along with each other?"

She said, "Oh, I don't know."

I asked, "Do you have any thoughts about what we can do to make this better?"

She said, "Oh, I don't know."

Then I asked, "Well, what keeps you going? What is your hope?"

She said, "Oh, I don't know." And then she turned away and, with deflated shoulders and heavy steps, walked into the other room. Outside, tensions between races were ripping at our city.

I went into my home office, shut the door, and wept like a baby for thirty minutes, wondering, *What can I do? I'm just one man.*

Not knowing what else to do, I prayed, "Lord, I belong to you. Is there something that you would like me to do? I need to do something to respond to this situation." I didn't say, "What does loyalty to Jesus Christ look like?" as I would today, but that's basically what I prayed.

Sometimes we choose our issues, but more often our issues choose us.

An idea began to take shape. Having seen the power of relationships to change minds (i.e., mine) about race, and with the help of a black professor at Rollins College, I invited forty men—twenty black and twenty white—to gather one Saturday morning on campus. The invitation wasn't to try to change Orlando but to see if we could change ourselves just by getting to know each other. Like Tom and I had done.

The attendance numbers were interesting. Of the forty men who were invited, exactly half showed up. Of the twenty men who showed up, exactly half were black and half were white—ten and ten.

Then, over the course of the morning, it became clear we had two mind-sets at this meeting. Of the twenty men in attendance, half wanted to go "do" something, change things, get involved in the political structure, pass laws, etc. The other half were saying, "No, no, no. We don't even know each other. Let's slow down here and get to know each other first and then see what happens."

Because I was under the influence of Tom Skinner, toward the end of the meeting I succeeded in steering the group to adopt a relationship-based approach. Then, out of the twenty men, ten dropped out.

Now we had ten men left, exactly half black and half white— five and five. For the next five years, we met one Saturday morning each month from 8:30 a.m. to noon, though we rarely ended on time. The group grew, and sometimes we had as many as twenty-five men present.

Interestingly, I didn't think I was a racist and would have fought against that idea—until we started meeting. But once we started meeting regularly, sometimes I would find myself saying, "You've got to be kidding me. That's just so ridiculous." Then a black guy would poke back. Sometimes a white guy would poke back too. There's a lot of poking that went on. We were starting to peel back the layers.

One month, we would have a smooth meeting and I would think, *He loves me.* But the next month, things would get cantankerous and I would think, *He loves me not.* But here's the point. We all kept coming back to the table. We were committed to redeeming this broken corner of our city's culture for the glory of God. And God changed us.

We came to care deeply about each other. And then came trust. Though we didn't start out to "do" anything, serving each other was inevitable—because that's what Christ's love brings out. We helped men start full-time ministries. We put two men through seminary. We put a roof on one of the brother's houses. Many practical needs were met. Seventeen of us went on a weekend retreat to North Carolina.

A former commander of the Black Liberation Army once came to a meeting to see if we were for real, and then he proceeded to overdose on drugs. The next thing I can remember is me, a white businessman, racing through the streets of downtown Orlando like a madman to rush an African American tough guy to the ER because of the reconciling power of God's love.

When it comes to racial reconciliation, that's an example of what loyalty to Jesus Christ looks like. What does it look like for you?

Because of the intense focus on racial reconciliation by Christians over the last several decades, a whole new generation of Christians are willing to break with the past and be reconciled with their Christian brothers.

Are you one of those men? Or would you like to be?

I've heard both black and white people say, "They'll never change. There must be another agenda. You can't trust those people." Or, "Oh well, I tried. I guess they just aren't interested."

Where does that kind of labeling and resignation come from? Certainly not from Jesus Christ. More importantly, how can we personally move beyond this kind of stereotyping? The Bible tells us how.

Paul wrote 1 Corinthians because a man was involved in sinful behavior. Paul told them to remove the brother from the fellowship. But when he wrote 2 Corinthians, he said, "The punishment inflicted on him by the majority is sufficient. Now instead, you ought to forgive and comfort him, so that he will not be overwhelmed by excessive sorrow. I urge you, therefore, to reaffirm your love for him" (2 Corinthians 2:6–8).

Men, is it time for you to move from 1 Corinthians to 2 Corinthians? Here's a call to action if you would like to personally do something about it—a proven idea that started in Mississippi.

A CALL TO ACTION: THREE-WEEK RECONCILIATION CHALLENGE

Tom Skinner said, "The problem is we do not know each other." If you are serious about racial reconciliation, invite one person of another color to meet with you once a week for three weeks with no other agenda except to get to know one another.

You can do this over lunch, breakfast, or coffee. Begin by asking each other to share how you each became followers of Jesus Christ and what God is doing in your life today. Exchange information about each other's families, work, and other interests.

If you are making progress, continue meeting with your new friend beyond three weeks. Can you picture what could happen in your community if you and another few dozen men would take this personal step? Your community would never be the same! This is the kind of reconciliation that is in the heart of God.

What else do we need to know?

It won't be easy.

Wherever you feel your community needs to be redeemed, wherever you take action to reclaim some broken part of culture, it's going to be hard. Otherwise, that problem would have been solved by now.

Jesus didn't labor under any illusion that engaging and redeeming culture would be easy: "I am sending you out like sheep among wolves. Therefore be as shrewd as snakes and as innocent as doves. Be on your guard; you will be handed over to the local councils and be flogged in the synagogues" (Matthew 10:16–17).

He also described the world as a place where God allows good and evil to coexist. Jesus explained a parable in which weeds (evil people) were allowed to grow next to wheat (good people) because pulling the weeds might accidentally uproot some of the wheat.

God knows the weeds are there. God knows the wolves and snakes are there.

Jesus didn't go looking for trouble, but he found it anyway. We should not go looking for trouble, but neither should we be surprised when we suffer for being Christians in an often hostile and wacky world.

Dear friends, do not be surprised at the fiery ordeal that has come on you to test you, as though something strange were happening to you.

1 Peter 4:12

"I have told you these things, so that in me you may have peace. In this world you will have trouble. But take heart! I have overcome the world."

John 16:33

"Therefore do not worry about tomorrow, for tomorrow will worry about itself. Each day has enough trouble of its own."

Matthew 6:34

Jesus knowingly sends us into a world he knows is inhospitable. Why? Because he has other children living with the mentality of a zoo lion who need to be set free.

Engaging the cultural issues of our day is going to be hard, but it will be worth it. We are on the right side of this. Where every other human ingenuity eventually fails, Jesus prevails.

THE NEED: MORE DANIELS IN BABYLON

God preserved the story of Joseph, who rose to a very high position in the secular Egyptian government for a reason. God preserved the story of Mordecai, who rose to a very high position in the secular government of Persia for a reason. And God preserved the story of Daniel, who also rose to a high position in the empire of Babylon for a reason. These men, who lived in three very different secular cultures, give us examples of how we too can live for the glory of God in a secular culture.

Consider Daniel, who distinguished himself as an administrator at an early age during the Babylonian captivity. Because of Daniel's exceptional abilities, King Darius planned to put him over all his other officials. In fact, it was their jealousy that led to Daniel getting thrown into the den of lions, which he survived. Daniel went on to prosper during the reigns of Darius and then Cyrus.

In many ways the church of Christ today is in a type of Babylonian captivity. Like the Jews in Babylon, we have a great deal of freedom. Like Daniel, many Christians have ranking positions. We need more Daniels of Babylon—men willing to go "into the world" and faithfully represent God in the culture.

Personally, I've always been fascinated by the possibility of influencing culture for the glory of Christ. Soon after becoming a follower of Jesus, six of us in our twenties who knew each other from business and church started a men's small group that met at my office. Here's a more detailed version of the story I told in *How God Makes Men*.

One morning, I invited our group to breakfast at IHOP and unveiled my big plan. I said, "We're all going to be impacting our families, churches, and businesses for Christ anyway. But how can we deeply impact our city for Christ? I would like to propose we fan out and each take a position in either politics, education, or civic life.

"Since I don't have children yet and am apolitical by nature," I said, "I volunteer to get involved in civic life." I joined the Winter Park Chamber of Commerce. Winter Park is a suburb of Orlando.

After a couple of Chamber meetings, I said, "Is there anything I can do around here to help?"

"Well, we need more people to serve on the program committee," came the reply. So, they put me on the program committee.

After a couple of meetings, the program committee chair

resigned. They said, "Would you like to chair the program committee?"

I said, "Sure."

Over the next year, we put on a robust program of monthly meetings with valuable topics that drew excellent crowds. I knew in my heart those meetings were strengthening our business culture. I knew those meetings had intrinsic value.

However, the reason I joined the Chamber in the first place—to represent Christ to the culture—was always in the back of my mind, and I wanted to make a bolder statement.

One morning I prayed, "God, would you please rehearse why you have me here? Could you please show me how we can have a bigger impact on our city's culture?" Or, in so many words, what does loyalty to Jesus Christ look like? No immediate answer.

Then one day not long after, God put the idea into my mind: "Why don't you see if the Winter Park Chamber program committee would like to put on a citywide prayer breakfast for the greater Orlando area on the Friday before Thanksgiving?" We already had a Mayor's Prayer Breakfast in the spring, but nothing spiritual on the community's fall calendar.

I said, "Okay, God, I'll give it a try." At our next program committee meeting, the response to my proposal was overwhelmingly positive. Because the previous year's programs had been excellent, my reputation was growing, and the idea sailed through the Chamber's executive committee and board of directors.

We named it the Thanksgiving Prayer Breakfast and invited one of Central Florida's most visible businessmen, Scott Linder, to be our speaker. Scott was a huge Florida Gator fan who regularly landed his blue-and-orange-Gator-accented helicopter on the lawn at the Florida Gas Company headquarters in Winter Park, where he served on the board of directors. He was practically a household name.

There was excitement as the guests began to arrive at a famous hotel where we held our first event. The food and service were terrific, and Mr. Linder recounted a riveting faith story. At the end of his message, he offered an invitation for anyone so inclined to commit or recommit themselves to faith in Jesus for salvation, and about 70 of the 150 or so guests did just that.

The impact on our community was palpable, so we decided to make it an annual event. The visibility of the prayer breakfast helped make it "okay" to be an openly Christian executive, business owner, banker, educator, judge, lawyer, politician, doctor, accountant, realtor, salesperson, contractor, etc. Many quiet Christians gained confidence to come out of the closet. Thousands of men and women surrendered and re-surrendered their lives to Jesus at the annual events.

While it's hard to measure cultural impact, some would say the Thanksgiving Prayer Breakfast was a unifying annual event for our entire city. It became an important and highly visible date on the community calendar.

THE CHALLENGE

How about you? Could God be calling you to be like a Daniel in Babylon, a Joseph in Egypt, or a Mordecai in Persia?

Here's the challenge for the next generation of Christian men: God is looking for men willing to be sent and to engage with and redeem civic affairs, the education system, public service, commerce, manufacturing, service industries, the justice system, education, the military, government, first responders, health care, medicine, the trades, and every other arena for the glory of Jesus Christ.

Will you be that man? Let that be your call to action for this chapter.

Where is the sting of the lack of the gospel most keenly felt in your community?

What is the unredeemed corner of culture in your community that needs to be claimed or reclaimed for the glory of Christ?

For the cultural issue that's burning on your mind, what would loyalty to Jesus Christ look like?

The Hopi Indians have a saying: "We are the ones we have been waiting for." Can you say that of yourself, for your community?

In our final chapter, we'll expand from engaging culture to authentically sharing our faith with the people we engage. Now it's time to close with a prayer and reflect on the questions.

Heavenly Father, first of all, thank you for showing us the example of how Jesus thought about culture. Help us to think about what one man can do, how we might be a Daniel in our own Babylon. What is the unredeemed corner of my community's culture that you want me to claim or reclaim for the glory of Christ? We pray that you would help each of us be loyal to the thoughts that you, by your Holy Spirit, put into our hearts and minds. We pray this in your name, Jesus Christ. Amen.

Reflection and Small Group Discussion Questions

1. What cultural issues are important to you, and why? Do you feel you're as engaged as you want to be, and why or why not?

2. What stance toward culture did Jesus take—embrace, withdraw, overthrow, replace, or engage? How would you describe the stance toward culture to which Jesus calls the Christian man?

3. Do you feel challenged to be more engaged? If so, take the challenge to find some unredeemed corner of culture and claim or reclaim it for the glory of Christ. Where is the sting of the lack of the gospel most keenly felt in your community?

TEN

SHARING MY FAITH

Having Authentic Spiritual Conversations with My Friends

We are therefore Christ's ambassadors, as though
God were making his appeal through us.

2 CORINTHIANS 5:20

> We're not trying to trick people into
> becoming Christians. Evangelism
> is simply taking someone as far
> as they want to go toward Jesus
> at that particular moment.

One day at the gym, I was lifting near a gigantic, hairy specimen of a man curling forty-five-pound dumbbells in anger like they were plastic props on a movie set. The pulsating veins in his bulging biceps looked like they would burst at any moment. He was a beast. A ferocious, mean-looking dude. Nobody was willing to venture within twenty-five feet of him.

As I finished my set and was putting my twenty-five-pound dumbbells back on the weight rack, Hercules was putting back his forty-fives. But instead of racking his weights in the correct place, he dropped them in the slots marked for the twenties.

Our eyes met. He scowled and gave me "the look," just daring me to say something.

I didn't want to embarrass him in front of everyone, so I let it go.

Okay, so maybe that's not really why. But to be serious, I didn't say anything because I genuinely pictured him getting violent. After staring me down with that withering look, he turned and walked away.

And then the strangest thing happened. I was completely overcome and enveloped with a love and compassion for this man. I just sensed he was in so much pain that his life was barely bearable. As he walked away, I prayed that God would help him.

How does that even happen?

THE BIG PICTURE

Every Christian man knows he should share his faith. Not many do. As one man said, "Sharing my faith scares and intimidates me." But that doesn't mean it doesn't weigh on him.

That's why so many of us want to know, "How can I acquire boldness in spreading the gospel? What are some practical ways I can share my faith at work? What is a great way to break the ice with people?"

In the chapter on friendships, I described how the world is a never-sleeping juggernaut that crushes everything in its path without pity and takes its toll on men. We need to be aware that most men are much more fragile than we would ever imagine—certainly far more vulnerable than they would ever want us to know. For this reason, in this chapter we will emphasize that evangelism is, at its core, a ministry of reconciliation. We need to treat people with love, kindness, empathy, and respect.

The big idea for this chapter is that we're not trying to trick people into becoming Christians. Evangelism is simply taking someone as far as they want to go toward Jesus at that particular moment. We do this because Jesus loves them and wants them to live with him in eternity. As his ambassadors, we are commissioned by him to broker the deal.

Remember our theme verse from chapter 1 on identity?

Therefore, if anyone is in Christ, the new creation has come:
The old has gone, the new is here!
2 Corinthians 5:17

The verses immediately following explain that we are the ones God has entrusted with both the *ministry* and the *message* that can make that happen!

All this is from God, who reconciled us to himself through Christ and gave us *the ministry of reconciliation:* that God was reconciling the world to himself in Christ, not counting people's sins against them. And he has committed to us *the message of reconciliation.*

We are therefore Christ's ambassadors, as though God were making his appeal through us. *We implore you on Christ's behalf: Be reconciled to God.*

2 Corinthians 5:18–20, emphasis added

In this chapter, you'll learn, or be reminded of, how we do the ministry of reconciliation. We'll discuss why we share our faith, how to start spiritual conversations, how to share your own spiritual story, and how to authentically help others change their lives in Christ. You'll feel your confidence surging as you acquire the tools—and mind-set—that will empower you to share your faith.

First, let's remind ourselves of the mission.

THE GREAT COMMISSION

In the chapter on spiritual growth (chapter 3), we looked at the last words of Jesus—the Great Commission—from the perspective of our own growth. Now it's time to look at them again—this time to understand our role as ambassadors in the ministry and message of reconciliation.

"Therefore go and make disciples of all nations, baptizing them in the name of the Father and of the Son and of the Holy Spirit, and teaching them to obey everything I have commanded you. And surely I am with you always, to the very end of the age."

Matthew 28:19–20

"But you will receive power when the Holy Spirit comes on you; and you will be my witnesses in Jerusalem, and in all Judea and Samaria, and to the ends of the earth."

Acts 1:8

This is the *mission*. These are our marching orders. They've never been amended, rescinded, or altered in any way. Making disciples is God's designated way to release the power of his gospel on all the issues that men face. Consider Troy.

WHY DO WE CARE?

Troy was released into a halfway house. Steve Basht, an area director with Man in the Mirror, led him and a group of men through an eight-week study of a Christian book. At thirty-seven years old, Troy had been addicted and incarcerated off and on since the age of fifteen. He was legendary for his barroom brawls and fierce temper. When asked, "How has this study affected you?" Troy said:

> I used to be the biggest piece of trash in town. I was either high, drunk, or angry. Last week, I realized I'm a different man!
>
> My ex-wife was about to have a baby fathered by my best friend. In her hour of need, he abandoned her. I was going over to confront him, and I was going to kill him.
>
> As I pulled into his driveway, a peace came over me. My rage disappeared, and I felt the need to pray for him. I then went to my ex-wife and pledged my support to her and my kids, even the unborn son of my best friend.

I feel a love for my children and ex-wife that I can't explain. I love them with no expectation of getting anything in return. My four-year-old daughter looked very sad when I was leaving last week, and I asked, "What's wrong?"

She said, "I want my daddy . . . my new daddy." Even *she* sees how much I have changed.

I know God loves me and is there to guide me. I don't have to do it myself. I have a peace I've never had before.

We care so much about the mission because nothing we've ever seen or experienced even remotely compares to the power of the gospel to change men's lives, whether Troy or ourselves.

What do we do with all our pent-up passion?

Bill Bright, founder of Campus Crusade for Christ International, would often ask, "What is the greatest thing that has ever happened to you?" Then he would follow up with, "Given your answer, what is the greatest thing that you can do for someone else?"

Any man who answers the first question, "To receive Jesus Christ as my Savior and Lord," will answer the second, "Help others give their lives to Jesus too."

But before we discuss how to execute the ministry of reconciliation, we need to answer a few important questions. The culture has shifted, and we need to talk about it.

TIMELESS MESSAGE, RELEVANT METHOD

If you are reading this, you were raised in an education system in which truth is considered relative. Relativism is the belief that there's no absolute truth, and different people can have different views about what is moral or immoral. In what might be the first shot fired in the culture wars, in 1987 professor Allan Bloom wrote in *The Closing of the American Mind*:

> There is one thing a professor can be absolutely certain of: *almost every student entering the university believes, or says he believes, that truth is relative* . . . The students' backgrounds are as various as America can provide. Some are religious, some atheists; some are to the Left, some to the Right; some intend to be scientists, some humanists or professionals or businessmen; some are poor, some rich . . . *The danger they have been taught to fear from absolutism is not error but intolerance*. Relativism is necessary to openness; and this is the virtue, *the only virtue, which all primary education for more than fifty years* [now more than eighty years] *has dedicated itself to inculcating*. Openness—and the relativism that makes it the only plausible stance in the face of various claims to truth and various ways of life and kinds of human beings—is *the great insight of our times. The true believer is the real danger.* The study of history and of culture teaches that all the world was mad in the past; men always thought they were right, and that led to wars, persecutions, slavery, xenophobia, racism, and chauvinism. *The point is not to correct the mistakes and really be right; rather it is not to think you are right at all.*[1]

This openness—and its aversion to *any* claim of absolute truth—is a dominant value in today's culture. As a result, many men, including Christian men, feel profoundly confused by the "truth" claims of Christianity.

Most statements that claim to be absolutely true run the risk of being an automatic turnoff to the next generation. The point is that truth claims are simply not going to resonate with the person who doesn't believe that absolute truth is even knowable.

Christianity is true. We believe it's true. But can you prove that Christianity is true? I would argue that by using the rules of evidence you can—a preponderance of evidence, as in civil cases, but also beyond a reasonable doubt, as in criminal cases.

But to the man who doesn't think you can know the truth, you cannot prove that Christianity is true. You cannot prove that the Bible is true.

How can we convince a new generation of people that Christianity is true when they do not believe in absolute truth?

A NEW STARTING POINT

We're going to need a new starting point to reach the next generation.

"But wait!" you say. "Isn't the fact that Christianity is true the whole basis for reaching out?" Of course. If you're a Christian, you believe Christianity is true. That's why you believe it. But that's not the point. People do things for their own reasons. We all do. Every salesperson knows they need to ask enough questions to figure out, "Why is this person interested? What are they looking for?" Then—and not until then—can they help their prospect solve that problem.

Claiming absolute truth simply does not resonate in today's secular culture. That's why, in most cases, it's pointless to make our appeal on the basis of absolute truth.

You have heard and perhaps even repeated, "God said it. I believe it. That settles it." But do you think that really resonates in today's culture? Not a chance!

For the vast majority of people, such appeals simply no longer connect. It's no longer a relevant way of engaging most people. It's reactionary. A throwback. It communicates, "I'm old-fashioned.

I haven't kept up with the times. I'm irrelevant. But even so, I know what's best for you. And I don't care what you think—this is the right way."

We could embarrass them with clever one-liners. When they tell us, "There is no such thing as absolute truth," we could ask, "Are you absolutely sure?" But that only adds to the prejudice that "Christians are judgmental and not loving." And hasn't there already been too much of that anyway? The reality is that even if you're *right*, you're *wrong* if you don't say it in love.

I fear a lot of us get so amped-up that people don't find us safe. We come off like the converted smoker who finally quit and now knows what's best for everyone else. What if today's average man finds the way you share the gospel as kooky to him as you find the guy who needs a bath holding a sign that reads, "Repent!" kooky to you?

Theologian Reinhold Niebuhr once said, "Nothing is so incredible as an answer to an unasked question."[2] With that in mind, what are the questions that the next generation is asking for which the gospel of Jesus provides an answer?

While the next generation is not asking, "What is truth?" they are asking, "What is real? What is authentic?"

This shift from "true" to "real" is something we can work with. I first became aware of it in the strangest possible setting: seminary.

I took apologetics from Ron Nash, one of the great professors of all time. Apologetics is the study of how to prove or defend the Christian faith. During a long semester, Professor Nash took us through all the many arguments to prove the existence of God: the cosmological argument, the ontological argument, the teleological argument, epistemological arguments, worldviews, the miracles, and how to answer the problem of gratuitous evil. He was brilliant!

And then, on the last day of class, Professor Nash floored me. He said, "In the time we've been together, we have looked at all the traditional arguments to prove Christianity. And all of these arguments have gravitas. But I would also be doing you a disservice if I did not conclude this class by telling you that, in my own experience, *easily the most powerful argument for truth of Christianity is a changed life."*

Why is that? Because a changed life is something "real." *Your* changed life is something real. It's something that will resonate. It's something beyond dispute.

A Timeless Message

In all this, we're not trying to change the *message* of reconciliation. What we are trying to do is, in the spirit of Francis Schaeffer, change the *method* of the ministry of reconciliation:

> There are two things we need to grasp firmly as we seek to communicate the gospel . . .
>
> The first is that *there are certain unchangeable facts which are true. These have no relationship to the shifting tides. They make the Christian system what it is and if they are altered, Christianity becomes something else.* This must be emphasized because there are evangelical Christians today who, in all sincerity, are concerned with their lack of communication, but in order to bridge the gap they are tending to change what must remain unchangeable. If we do this, we are no longer communicating Christianity, and what we have left is no different from the surrounding consensus.[3]

Professor Nash was fond of saying, "I don't care if someone wants to invent a new religion. I just wish they wouldn't call it Christianity." We don't want to do that either.

We're going to stick with the unchangeable facts of the gospel message.

A Relevant Method

However, Schaeffer wasn't done. He continued:

> But we cannot present a balanced picture if we stop here. We must realize that *we are facing a rapidly changing historical situation, and if we are going to talk to people about the gospel we need to know what is the present ebb and flow of thought-forms. Unless we do this the unchangeable principles of Christianity will fall on deaf ears . . .*
>
> It is much more comfortable, of course, to go on speaking the gospel only in familiar phrases to the middle classes.[4]

In other words, how do we speak to rappers? To hipsters? To gays? How do we bring the gospel to them? And then possibly Schaeffer's most famous statement:

> Each generation of the church in each setting has the responsibility of communicating the gospel in understandable terms, considering the language and thought-forms of that setting . . .
>
> The reason we often cannot speak to our children, let alone other people's, is because we have never taken time to understand how different their thought-forms are from ours . . . In crucial areas, many Christian parents, ministers, and teachers are as out of touch with many of the children of the church, and the majority of those outside, as though they were speaking a foreign language.[5]

What's the saying about the definition of insanity? Doing the same thing over and over again and expecting a different result. While we never change the *message*, we should never hesitate to adjust our *methods*.

*Short version: For this generation, a more resonant starting point
is not that Christianity is true but that it's real.*

Again, we're not saying it's more important that Christianity
be real than true, only that it's a more resonant starting point to
a generation that can't grasp claims of absolute truth.

This is the first key to engage our audience: to understand
where they're coming from.

PEOPLE NEED A GUIDE

Our culture is in the middle of an excruciating and dramatic
mega-shift from a core set of values mostly informed by Christianity to a more pluralistic and constantly morphing jumble of
secular values.

As a result, as I said at the very beginning of this book, many
men feel profoundly confused. They're not sure what's expected
of them or how to make it happen. Many men, especially men
under forty, would be hard-pressed to explain what the word
man even means. A man is created to love God and others, and
to lead, serve, protect, and provide for his family and community.
When a man doesn't understand these roles, or understands but
neglects them, everyone suffers. The collateral damage has been
staggering in their marriages, families, friendships, the workplace,
and communities—*your* community.

They need what only the Lord Jesus Christ has to offer.

They also need a guide.

Blue Like Jazz author Donald Miller, in his business book
Building a StoryBrand, has created an incredible summary of what
happens in every story worth telling: "A CHARACTER who
wants something encounters a PROBLEM before they can get it.
At the peak of their despair, a GUIDE steps into their lives, gives

them a PLAN, and CALLS THEM TO ACTION. That action plan helps them avoid FAILURE and ends in a SUCCESS."[6]

You and I—we are the guides. As guides, we need two things: (1) someone in despair who needs a guide, and (2) a plan of action that leads that person to reconciliation with Christ and the people they love.

What follows is a step-by-step process to help a person change their life in Christ. First, we'll discuss how to break the ice and start a spiritual conversation. Then I'll give you a proven, time-tested way to share your spiritual story. Finally, I'll give you what you need to help someone become a Christian.

STARTING SPIRITUAL CONVERSATIONS: THE GOLDEN QUESTION

The best method of evangelism is the one you will actually use. That said, let me tell you what I do, because I've been fine-tuning my approach across four decades.

When I see a hurting man—and they're easy to spot—I ask the Lord what I'm supposed to do. Sometimes it's simply to say a quick prayer, but often it's to ask, "Would you like to grab a cup of coffee?"

I've discovered one cup of coffee can change the world!

My method revolves around a Golden Question that I've asked several thousand men in one-on-one situations. Often I ask it over coffee, but it also could be a meal, during a first-time visit to our Bible study, at the gym, or when I'm paying the bill to a serviceman for home repairs.

Occasionally I start with this question, but usually it's after I've broken the ice with questions about their work and family. To keep it short, I tend not to ask follow-up questions.

Then, usually within three minutes, I ask the Golden Question: *"Where are you on your spiritual journey?"*

It's virtually a perfect question because everyone has given their spirituality some thought. And who doesn't enjoy talking about themselves?

All have been eager to respond. No doubt a big part of their willingness is my mind-set and attitude. I have a nonthreatening and nonjudgmental smile on my face. Men can sense I'm sincere and really want their answer. I try to give the signal that I want the (1) long and (2) *real* answer.

I don't use the Golden Question as a trick. I really want to know. Invariably they mention something that I've been through myself. Then it can become a dialogue—although I move very slowly in order to not violate the process of relationships. And I never act like I have all the answers, because I really don't think I do.

Every now and then, of course, our coffee time ends up as just a seed on the rocky path. But usually it's something they have given a lot of thought to—cable repair guys, auto technicians, gym acquaintances, seatmates on planes, work acquaintances, you name it.

"Where are you on your spiritual journey?" Will you ask one person you meet over the next twenty-four hours this question? Would that be a good call to action for you?

I predict you will like it. The Golden Question over a cup of coffee can bring a fresh, new dimension to your personal ministry.

After you get the answer to the Golden Question, what's next?

SHARING YOUR STORY:
YOUR 3-MINUTE ELEVATOR STORY

Now it's your turn. We'll get to that momentarily, but first a caution.

Red alert: After you hear a man's story, your mind will likely be exploding with all kinds of terrific information that can "fix" him. Resist that urge! Instead of regaling him with your theological knowledge, put a lid on it. Christianity is a religion of propositional truth, but at this early stage, you haven't earned the right to share it.

The man across from you doesn't care about how much you know. He wants to know if you're for real. Remember, for this generation, a more resonant starting point is that Christianity is real. The 3-Minute Elevator Story Worksheet is a time-tested, proven way to get real.

With that in mind, what can we say that will open the minds of the next generation to the gospel?

> Always be prepared to give an answer to everyone who asks you to give the reason for the hope that you have. But do this with gentleness and respect.
>
> *1 Peter 3:15*

After you've listened carefully, tell him where you are on your spiritual journey by adapting your 3-Minute Elevator Story that you've prepared in advance, using the following guide.

HOW TO PREPARE A 3-MINUTE ELEVATOR STORY

Use this worksheet to prepare a 3-minute "elevator speech" of your faith story (testimony). Time it to about one minute for each of the three sections. You can always talk longer if you have more time, but by doing it this way, you'll "always be prepared" (1 Peter 3:15).

BEFORE (150 words): What was your life like before you embraced Jesus? Empty, confused, lonely, disillusioned, futile, lacking significance, without purpose or meaning, discontent, successful but still not happy? As much as possible, relate your story to what you know about their story.

_____
_____
_____
_____
_____

HOW (150 words): How did you come to profess faith in Jesus? Where? Who showed you the way? Why did you respond? As prompted, mention the love and holiness of God, being convicted of your sins, hungering for something real, understanding who Christ is, desiring eternal life, asking Jesus to forgive your sins, and having faith in Jesus.

_____
_____
_____
_____
_____

AFTER (150 words): What has Christ done in your life since? Pick areas that have changed which relate to the person's struggles.

_____
_____
_____
_____
_____

Can you picture a previous encounter when it would have made a difference if you had prepared and memorized this 3-Minute Elevator Story?

If you're serious about sharing Christ with people—or want to be—don't shoot from the hip. Photocopy the worksheet. Take a couple of hours to write out, time, practice, and memorize your 3-Minute Elevator Story. Pick words that sparkle and emote. Mark Twain said, "A powerful agent is the right word."[7] And you already know what happens to the athlete who doesn't practice.

SHARING JESUS' STORY

Hopefully the person you're building rapport with will resonate and connect with your story. Step 1 is asking the Golden Question. Step 2 is sharing your 3-Minute Elevator Story. Step 3 is to share the story of Jesus, the good news, or gospel, about Jesus. But what does that mean?

Oswald Chambers wrote:

It is not the strength of one man's personality being superimposed on another, but the real presence of Christ coming through the elements of the worker's life. When we preach *the historic facts of the life and death of Our Lord as they are conveyed in the New Testament,* our words are made sacramental; God uses them on the ground of His Redemption to create in those who listen that which is not created otherwise . . .

If a man attracts by his personality, his appeal is along that line; if he is identified with his Lord's personality, then the appeal is along the line of what Jesus Christ can do. The danger is to glory in men; Jesus says we are to lift *Him* up.[8]

Writing and readability expert Rudolf Flesch has been quoted as saying, "There is nothing truly readable but a story." Our faith does consist of propositions—direct statements about what we believe. And we believe these propositions are true. But in most cases, reciting propositional truth isn't what connects in any generation, much less the current generation. It's *the story*: "the historic facts of the life and death of Our Lord as they are conveyed in the New Testament," as Chambers put it.

One hundred years ago, Princeton Seminary professor and author Gresham Machen noted that exhorting people about how they ought to live has never succeeded in transforming men's lives:

> The strange thing about Christianity was that it adopted an entirely different method. It transformed the lives of men not by appealing to the human will, but *by telling a story*; not by exhortation, but by *the narration of an event*. It is no wonder that such a method seemed strange. Could anything be more impractical than the attempt to influence conduct by rehearsing events concerning the death of a religious teacher? . . . But the strange thing is that it works . . . Where the most eloquent exhortation fails, *the simple story of an event succeeds; the lives of men are transformed by a piece of news*.[9]

How, then, after telling your own story do you present the story of Jesus?

THREE ESSENTIAL IDEAS

There are so many ways to present the gospel of Jesus, and no single right way. As the Holy Spirit leads, tell about Jesus' birth, his life, his teachings, his ministry, his miracles, his death, and his resurrection. Focus on who he is, why he came, and what belief in him means.

Men will have many questions, but in my experience, those questions fall by the wayside when we bring them into contact with the real Jesus. As Chambers said above, "Our words are made sacramental; God uses them on the ground of His Redemption to create in those who listen that which is not created otherwise."

That said, here are three focusing ideas you can use to help people understand the gospel, adapted from the work of Bill Bright:

- *God loves you very much.*

    "For God so loved the world that he gave his one and only Son, that whoever believes in him shall not perish but have eternal life" (John 3:16).
- *Jesus died to forgive our sins and to give us eternal life, purpose, and meaning.*

    "You see, at just the right time, when we were still powerless, Christ died for the ungodly" (Romans 5:6).

    "Here is a trustworthy saying that deserves full acceptance: Christ Jesus came into the world to save sinners" (1 Timothy 1:15).

    "I have come that they may have life, and have it to the full" (John 10:10).

    "For it is by grace you have been saved, through faith— and this is not from yourselves, it is the gift of God—not by works, so that no one can boast" (Ephesians 2:8–9).
- *We become Christians when we personally confess our sins and believe in Jesus.*

    "If we confess our sins, he is faithful and just and will forgive us our sins and purify us from all unrighteousness" (1 John 1:9).

"If anyone acknowledges that Jesus is the Son of God, God lives in them and they in God" (1 John 4:15).

"Yet to all who did receive him, to those who believed in his name, he gave the right to become children of God" (John 1:12).

"If you declare with your mouth, 'Jesus is Lord,' and believe in your heart that God raised him from the dead, you will be saved" (Romans 10:9).

ASK THE PLATINUM QUESTION

Let's retrace what we've discussed so far. Step 1 is to ask the Golden Question, "Where are you on your spiritual journey?" Step 2 is to share your own 3-Minute Elevator Story. Step 3 is to share the story of Jesus—the good news, or gospel, about Jesus.

Now it's time for step 4, which is to ask the Platinum Question. But before you ask, there's something of extraordinary importance you will want to know.

A lot of people really care deeply about this person who sits in front of you—wives, children, fathers, mothers, brothers, sisters, friends. They have poured out their lives, hearts, and prayer for this very moment.

Not only that, but the Holy Spirit has been sovereignly orchestrating all the seemingly random circumstances of this person's life to bring them to this moment.

For these reasons, many people are ready to become Christians *right now*. They are ready, willing, and able, but no one has ever actually asked them this Platinum Question:

"Have you ever personally confessed your sins and put your faith in Jesus?"

To not ask this question would be like you walking into a car showroom, drooling over a car, and after thirty minutes of talking it over with a salesperson, hearing them say, "I can see you're really interested in this car. Tell you what. Why don't you give me your name and phone number and I'll call you in a couple of weeks to see if you're still interested?"

The salesperson would have missed their moment.

So please, ask this question! What comes next will last forever.

THE FINAL STEP: A PRAYER OF FAITH

If they say yes, then say, "That's wonderful! How [or when] did that happen?" You do this because you want to make sure you are both talking about the same thing.

If they say no, then simply (with no embellishment or qualifications) ask, "Would you like to right now?"

If they say no, then say, "I understand. Let's keep talking in the days ahead. I would love to help you in any way I can."

If they say yes, then say, "In that case, you can pray right now and invite Jesus into your life. Would you like to do that?"

The answer will invariably be yes, so then say, "Okay, let's bow our heads and pray."

Here a prayer you can pray out loud, one phrase at a time, asking them to repeat after you:

Lord Jesus, I need You.

I believe you love me and came to die for my sins.

I am filled with a deep sorrow for my sins.

By grace through faith, I receive you as my Savior and Lord.

Please forgive my sins and save my soul.

Thank you for your forgiveness, the gift of eternal life, and the promise of life to the full.

Please change me into the person you created me to become. Amen.

If this prayer is too much for you, it can be as simple as the nine words on the best billboard I've ever seen: "Jesus, please forgive my sins and save my soul." Nine words that capture the true essence of reconciliation with God.

If you just can't get comfortable praying for salvation with someone, bring along someone who is more experienced to help you.

Congratulate them. Ask them to share what they just did with another Christian. Describing it to another person will help them further conceptualize what they've just done. And the positive feedback will affirm them in their decision.

End your time together by suggesting some next steps, such as telling their spouse (if they have one), telling their pastor (if they have one), attending church or joining you for church, becoming part of a Bible study, or getting a Bible and starting with the four gospels (eighty-nine chapters, so perhaps one chapter a day for three months).

Best idea: If it's a man, take him under your wing and show him the ropes. You could take him through this book one chapter per week.

LET'S REVIEW

So let's review. Here's a summary of the practical steps you can take to be the "guide" who brings both the *ministry* and *message* of reconciliation to people in despair when they're ready for "a plan that calls them to action."

- First, start spiritual conversations by asking the Golden Question: *"Where are you on your spiritual journey?"* Let them see the life of Christ exemplified in you as you show a personal interest in them.
- Second, share your personal faith story—your 3-Minute Elevator Story.
- Third, tell them about the story of Jesus and his gospel—including the three essential ideas: God loves you; Jesus came to forgive sins and give eternal life; and we become Christians when we personally confess our sins and put our faith in Jesus.
- Fourth, ask them the Platinum Question: *"Have you ever personally confessed your sins and put your faith in Jesus?"*
- Fifth, when they are ready, help them pray a prayer of faith and invite Jesus into their life: *"Jesus, please forgive my sins and save my soul."*

YOU ARE MAKING AN ETERNAL DIFFERENCE

Making disciples is the one idea that, once fully understood and truly believed, changes everything. Marriages, families, the workplace, our communities, our country. Everything.

Have you heard the story about the little boy throwing a starfish back into the sea? Someone said, "You're wasting your time. That isn't going to make any difference." But the little boy picked up a starfish, threw it back into the surf, and said, "Well, it made a difference for that one."

Helping people change their lives in Christ makes an eternal difference. So engage, because if the Great Commission is true, our plans are not too big; they're too small.

Our dearest Father, we are men who are passionate to authentically share our faith. Lord, our deepest conviction is that your gospel does change lives, and we have a deep conviction to do something about it. Help us to channel our passion to authentically help people change their lives. We humbly accept our commission as ambassadors of Christ who bring the ministry and the message of reconciliation to a broken, hurting world. Give us boldness to ask the Golden Question, share our 3-Minute Elevator Story, tell the story of Jesus, ask the Platinum Question, and help people invite Jesus Christ into their lives. We ask this, Jesus, in your name. Amen.

Reflection and Small Group Discussion Questions

1. What has been the best experience you've ever had sharing your faith, and what made it so good?

2. What is our *mission* as described in Matthew 28:18–20 and Acts 1:8? What is our *ministry* and *message* as described in 2 Corinthians 5:18–20?

3. How do you personally go about sharing your faith? How has your style of being an "ambassador" been working? What has been discussed in this chapter that can equip and inspire you to have more authentic spiritual conversations with your friends (e.g., the Golden Question, your 3-Minute Elevator Story, the Three Essential Ideas, the Platinum Question, the Prayer of Faith)? What is your personal call to action?

AFTERWORD

As the wild lion mentored the zoo lion about the glories of the jungle, I've been discipling you in this book about the glories of walking with Christ.

This may surprise you, but you now know as much as anyone about what it means to be a Christian man. There is no "secret" knowledge about how to be a man. You have everything you need to passionately love God, protect and provide for your family, treat others well, find satisfying work, and courageously stay the course while experiencing contentment, peace, and joy.

For the ten issues presented in this book, we explored a big idea that, fully understood and genuinely believed, can change everything. To wrap it up, here they are again, along with each chapter's call to action:

Identity: When you seek your identity in Jesus Christ and his gospel, you will find a deep, lasting satisfaction so infectious that others will want it too. For your call to action, pray "My Declaration of Christian Manhood."

Life Balance: You have all the time you need to do everything God wants you to do. For your call to action, set aside two or three hours for a personal retreat and drill down on what you want your priorities to be.

Growth: A Bible, a small group, and serving someone else will solve 90 percent of your problems. For your call to action, read the Bible for yourself, be part of a small group, and serve someone else.

Marriage: Most marriage problems would disappear if we would simply speak to our wives with the same kindness, courtesy, forethought, and respect with which we speak to our coworkers. Your call to action has four parts—the 70 percent mind-set, praying for and with your wife, the emotional bank account, and making your wife your best friend.

Children: "Yes, I love you, and no, you can't have your own way." Your call to action is to implement several of these practical ideas: love their mother well, disciple your children, lead family devotions, pay for personal devotions, take to church, spend time, set boundaries, give time the way they want it, date them as teens, eat dinner together, pray for them, and encourage them with words.

Friendships: What's really going to help you long-term is to find a friend or two, or join a small group, and live life together with a few brothers with whom you can process what comes your way. For your call to action, join or start a men's small group.

Work: There is no greater feeling than to believe, "This is what I'm supposed to be doing, right here, right now—even if it's hard." Your call to action is to answer these questions: How are you wired? What does that tell you about yourself, and about the types of positions that would satisfy you in the long term? What are your social needs? What are your health/stress needs? What is your long-term vocational goal? Assuming time and money are no object, what would you do if you could do anything you wanted? Why would you not do it?

Lust: The practical solution to lust (and other sexual immoral-ity) for most men is to get married and enjoy regular sex with their wife. For your call to action, make the covenant that Job made not to lust, make your own intentional plan following Miguel's model, and pray the prayer patterned on Ed Cole's prayer.

Culture: God wants each of us to go find some unredeemed corner of culture and claim it for the glory of Christ. Your call to action is to find some broken part of your community and allow God to send you to redeem it. And as God leads, take the three-week racial reconciliation challenge

Sharing Your Faith: We're not trying to trick people into becoming Christians. Evangelism is simply taking someone as far as they want to go toward Jesus at that particular moment. God has commissioned us as ambassadors to broker the deal. Your call to action is to have authentic spiritual conversations as you use the Golden Question ("Where are you on your spiritual journey?), your 3-Minute Elevator Story, the Three Essential Ideas, and the Platinum Question ("Have you ever personally confessed your sins and put your faith in Jesus?") and to help people pray the Prayer of Faith.

NOW WHAT?

As a final call to action, consider:

- coaching a man into biblical manhood
- getting coached by a more experienced Christian man
- studying the book in a new or existing small group

To start a new group, refer back to the section "How to Start and Sustain a Weekly Men's Small Group" on page 144.

For additional help, you can also download a complimentary digital copy of *The Christian Man Coaching Guide* at TheChristian ManBook.com.

As we part, remember, you can live a heroic life right now for the glory of Christ. This win is yours for the taking. So take it. You're free. I'll be praying for you.

ACKNOWLEDGMENTS

So many people have directly and indirectly contributed to make this book possible. I would especially like to thank a few of them by name.

Robert Tunmire, Jamie Turco, and John Vonberg provided valuable insights as my "first readers."

My colleagues at Man in the Mirror all deserve appreciation, and especially Kimberly Massari, my assistant; Brett Clemmer, our president; Bryan Richardson, for thinking through how this book can advance our mission; and Brian Russell, who came up with the brilliant idea of "the fingerprint man" for the cover.

Robert and Erik Wolgemuth are visionaries who saw the potential of this book and handled the myriad of publishing details that must be completed to bring a book to market.

And to my publisher, Zondervan, I am deeply grateful. The entire organization has gotten behind this book. I would especially like to express my gratitude and appreciation to David Morris, Andy Rogers, Dirk Buursma, Amanda Halash, Andrea Pancoast, Kait Lamphere, Curt Diepenhorst, Brandon

Henderson, Tom Dean, Trinity McFadden, Keith Finnegan, and Charlie Hubert, for their unique publishing roles in procuring, editing, designing, marketing, publicizing, and distributing *The Christian Man*.

PATRICK MORLEY BOOKS FOR INDIVIDUAL OR GROUP STUDY

The Man in the Mirror

Discover solutions for the twenty-four problems men face. Called by some the best book for men ever written. With four million copies in print, this book offers a life-changing look at how you can trade the rat race for the rewards of godly manhood. Discussion questions at the end of each chapter. Single copies at all retail outlets and cases of twelve and forty-eight available at booksbythebox.org.

Devotions for the Man in the Mirror

Learn how to surrender every area of your life to Christ. Seventy-five short readings, two to four pages each, each written to help you think more deeply about the God who is, escaping cultural Christianity, daily struggles, getting along with people, and more. A prayer at the end of each reading.

Devotions for Couples

Strengthen your intimacy as a couple in every conceivable area with 120 two-page devotional readings. Learn how to better understand each other, how to communicate, what pulls couples apart, how to stay together, and more. Discussion questions, applications, and a prayer for each devotion.

Seven Seasons of the Man in the Mirror

Find encouragement for the hidden dangers and opportunities for personal growth in each of the seven seasons of your life: Reflection, Building, Crisis, Renewal, Rebuilding, Suffering, and Success. Discussion questions at the end of each chapter.

Second Half for the Man in the Mirror

Practical ideas for twenty crucial concerns of men making a midlife transition. This book gives practical ideas for making the journey ahead even more fulfilling than the one behind. Discussion questions at the end of each chapter.

Man Alive

Find relief for the seven inner aches and pains that hold men back:

- I just feel like I'm in this alone.
- I don't feel like God cares about me personally.
- My life doesn't have purpose—it seems random.
- I have destructive behaviors dragging me down.
- My soul feels dry.
- My most important relationships aren't healthy.
- I'm not doing anything that will make a difference.

Discussion questions at the end of each chapter.

How God Makes Men

Discover ten powerful principles that will elevate you to a more biblical Christianity from ten well-known men in the Bible: Abraham, Joseph, Moses, Gideon, David, Solomon, Nehemiah, Job, Peter, and Paul. See the circumstances God used to mold and shape their lives, and find out how those principles are still at work today. Discussion questions at the end of each chapter.

A Man's Guide to the Spiritual Disciplines

Master twelve spiritual habits to keep your spiritual life robust and fully integrated with your daily life. Includes creation, the Bible, prayer, worship, the Sabbath, fellowship, counsel, fasting, spiritual warfare, stewardship, service, and evangelism. Discussion questions at the end of each chapter.

A Man's Guide to Work

Increase your workplace IQ with answers to questions about calling, purpose, integrity, performance, people at work, witnessing at work, money, priorities, praying for success, planning, leadership, and how to handle failure. Discussion questions at the end of each chapter.

The Young Man in the Mirror

Help your teens with this rite-of-passage book that will teach them what it means to be a man, how to get along with their family members, how to treat young women, how to handle sexual temptation, and how to find God's will for their lives. Great for fathers and sons to read and discuss the questions together. Excellent for groups of fathers and sons too.

Is Christianity for You?

Help a friend investigate the common objections to Christian belief with answers to tough questions like, "Is the idea of God logical?" "Shouldn't science rule over theology?" and "If God is good, why is there so much suffering?" Discussion questions at the end of each chapter. Single copies on Amazon.com and cases of twelve and forty-eight available at booksbythebox.org.

NOTES

Chapter 1: Identity: Settling Who I Am and What My Life Is About

1. C. S. Lewis, *God in the Dock* (Grand Rapids: Eerdmans, 1970), 202.
2. Lewis, *God in the Dock*, 202, emphasis original.
3. Blaise Pascal, *Pensées* (London: Penguin, 1966), 65–66.

Chapter 2: Life Balance: How to Be Faithful with Everything Entrusted to Me

1. See Paul Leinwand and Cesare Mainardi, "Stop Chasing Too Many Priorities," *Harvard Business Review*, April 14, 2011, https://hbr.org/2011/04/stop-chasing-too-many-prioriti.
2. "Warren Buffett's 5-Step Process for Prioritizing True Success (and Why Most People Never Do it)," Live Your Legend, February 1, 2011, https://liveyourlegend.net/warren -buffetts-5-step-process-for-prioritizing-true-success-and -why-most-people-never-do-it.
3. Graeme, "Thelema," The Will Project, March 14, 2011, https://willproject.org/history/thelema.
4. Cited in James A. Francis, "The Easter Faith," in *The Baptist* 1, no. 9 (March 27, 1920): 300.

5. Richard Foster, *Celebration of Discipline* (San Francisco: Harper & Row, 1978), 1.

6. John Calvin, *Institutes of the Christian Religion*, vol. 1, ed. John T. McNeill (Philadelphia: Westminster, 1960), 35.

7. Quoted in E. M. Bounds, *E. M. Bounds on Prayer*, ed. Harold Chadwick (Orlando, FL: Bridge-Logos, 2001), 608.

8. Mother Teresa, *A Simple Path* (New York: Ballantine, 1995), 79.

9. Howard Dayton, personal correspondence, May 26, 2018.

10. Brother Lawrence of the Resurrection, *The Practice of the Presence of God* (New York: Doubleday, 1977), 96.

11. Quoted in William R. Moody, *The Life of D. L. Moody by His Son* (1900; repr., Eugene, OR: Wipf and Stock, 2018), 319.

12. Bob Dylan, "Gotta Serve Somebody," Columbia Records, August 20, 1979.

13. Quoted in Richard Whately, *Bacon's Essays* (Boston: Lee and Shepard, 1868), 472.

Chapter 3: Growth: Becoming a More Kingdom-Minded Man

1. William R. Moody, *The Life of D. L. Moody by His Son* (1900; repr., Eugene, OR: Wipf and Stock, 2018), 134.

2. Patrick Morley, *A Man's Guide to the Spiritual Disciplines: 12 Habits to Strengthen Your Walk with Christ* (Chicago: Moody, 2007).

3. Oswald Chambers, *My Utmost for His Highest* (1935; repr., Uhrichsville, OH: Barbour, 1963), August 23rd, 173.

4. Robert Coleman, *The Master Plan of Evangelism*, 2nd ed. (1963; repr., Grand Rapids: Revell, 2010), 116.

5. Quoted in Donald Keys, *Earth at Omega: Passage to Planetization* (Boston: Branden, 1982), 79.

6. Carl Smith, personal correspondence; Kenneth O. Gangel, *Unwrap Your Spiritual Gifts* (Wheaton, IL: Victor, 1883); Leslie B. Flynn, *19 Gifts of the Spirit* (Wheaton, IL: Victor, 1974).

Chapter 4: Marriage: Finding a New Best Friend in My Wife

1. Quoted in Kristen Driscoll, "Ruth Bell Graham: A Life Well Lived, Part 2," *Decision*, June 2013, https://billygraham

.org/decision-magazine/june-2013/ruth-bell-graham-a-life
-well-lived-part-2.

2. Edwin H. Friedman, *Generation to Generation: Family Process in Church and Synagogue* (New York: Guilford, 1985), 69.

3. Gary Chapman, *The 5 Love Languages: The Secret to Love That Lasts* (Chicago: Northfield, 2015).

Chapter 5: Children: A Dad Who Really Makes a Difference

1. Pat Morley and David Delk, *The Dad in the Mirror: How to See Your Heart for God Reflected in Your Children* (Grand Rapids: Zondervan, 2003), 15.

2. See Murray Bowen, *Family Therapy in Clinical Practice* (Lanham, MD: Jason Aronson, 2002), 175–76.

3. Patrick Morley, *The Man in the Mirror: Solving the 24 Problems Men Face*, 25th anniv. ed. (1989; repr., Grand Rapids: Zondervan, 2014), 138–39.

Chapter 6: Friendships: Finding and Keeping Godly Friends

1. Patrick Morley, *Man Alive: Transforming Your 7 Primal Needs into a Powerful Spiritual Life* (Colorado Springs: Multnomah, 2012), 6–7.

Chapter 7: Work: How Should I Think about My Work?

1. "Mike Rowe: *Dirty Jobs* Reached Same People as Donald Trump's Campaign," *Meet the Press*, NBC News, December 11, 2016, www.youtube.com/watch?v=33h2mgrY_ZI.

Chapter 8: Lust: The Right Way to Deal with This Powerful Drive

1. G. K. Chesterton, *Orthodoxy* (New York: John Lane, 1908), 103.

2. See Alexis C. Madrigal, "How Often Men Think about Sex," *Atlantic*, June 23, 2014, www.theatlantic.com/technology/archive/2014/06/how-often-men-think-about-sex/373230.

3. See "Jacobellis v. Ohio," June 22, 1964, www.law.cornell
.edu/supremecourt/text/378/184.
4. Carl Thomas, "Three Ways to Look and Not Lust,"
September 11, 2018, www.xxxchurch.com/men/3-ways-to-
look-and-not-lust.html.
5. Edwin Louis Cole, *Maximized Manhood: A Guide to Family
Survival* (New Kensington, PA: Whitaker House, 1982), 15.

Chapter 9: Culture: The Role of a Christian Man in Our Culture

1. See Kahlil Gibran, "The Wise King," www.poetryfoundation
.org/poems/58702/the-wise-king.
2. Quoted in Aimee Millwood, "A Top TripAdvisor Reviewer Talks
about How Reviews Work, for Good and Bad," *Entrepreneur*,
July 15, 2016, www.entrepreneur.com/article/278954.
3. See Ralph L. Lewis and Gregg Lewis, *Learning to Preach Like
Jesus* (Westchester, IL: Crossway, 1989), 13.
4. Elizabeth Rundle Charles, *Chronicles of the Schönberg-Cotta
Family* (New York: T. Nelson, 1864), 276.

Chapter 10: Sharing My Faith: Having Authentic Spiritual Conversations with My Friends

1. Allan Bloom, *The Closing of the American Mind: How Higher
Education Has Failed Democracy and Impoverished the Souls of
Today's Students*, 25th anniv. ed. (1987; repr., New York: Simon &
Schuster, 2012), 25–26, emphasis and bracketed comment added.
2. Reinhold Niebuhr, Human Destiny (New York: Scribner's,
1943), 6.
3. Francis A. Schaeffer, *Escape from Reason* (1968; repr.,
Downers Grove, IL: InterVarsity, 2014), 119, emphasis added.
4. Schaeffer, *Escape from Reason*, 119–20, emphasis added.
5. Schaeffer, *Escape from Reason*, 120–21.
6. Donald Miller, *Building a StoryBrand: Clarify Your Message
So Customers Will Listen* (Nashville: HarperCollins
Leadership, 2017), 20.

7. Mark Twain, "William Dean Howells," in *What Is Man? and Other Essays* (New York: Harper, 1917), 229.

8. Oswald Chambers, *My Utmost for His Highest* (1935; repr., Uhrichsville, OH: Barbour, 1963), November 9th, emphasis added.

9. J. Gresham Machen, *Christianity and Liberalism*, rev. ed. (1923; repr., Grand Rapids: Eerdmans, 2009), 40, emphasis added.